52
NEW JERSEY
weekends

52
NEW JERSEY
weekends

Mitch Kaplan

COUNTRY ROADS PRESS
Oaks • Pennsylvania

Published by Country Roads Press
P.O. Box 838, 2170 West Drive
Oaks, PA 19456

Text design by Studio 3.
Illustrations by Dale Ingrid Swensson.
Map by Allen Crider.
Typesetting by Typeworks.

ISBN 1-56626-126-0

Library of Congress Cataloging-in-Publication Data

Kaplan, Mitch.
    52 New Jersey weekends / author, Mitch Kaplan ; illustrator,
Dale Ingrid Swensson.
        p.   cm.
    Includes index.
    ISBN 1-56626-126-0
    1. New Jersey–Tours.   I. Title.
F132.3.K36   1995
917.4904′43–dc20   95-15207
                                                                           CIP

Printed in the United States of America.
10 9 8 7 6 5 4 3 2 1

To Penny
for infinite patience

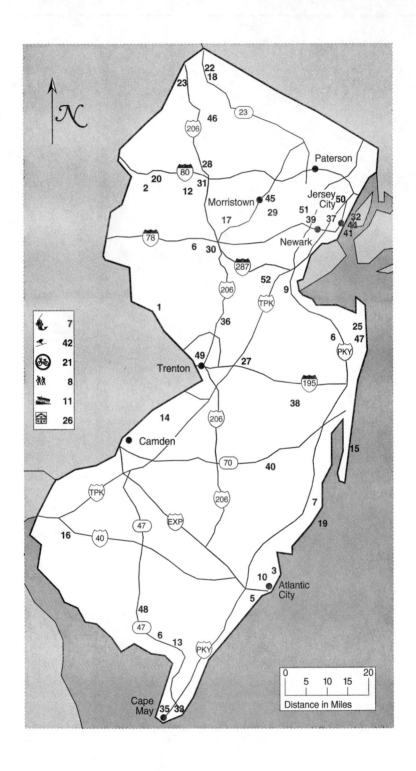

Contents

Spring

Summer

Fall

Winter

Introduction

To many people, New Jersey is nothing more than a toll road exit, an ugly industrial landscape off the Turnpike, or an overpopulated little place wedged between New York City and Philadelphia.

I grew up here, and I'm raising my kids here. Still, it wasn't until I began working on this book that I began to appreciate one very clear fact: New Jersey hides a wealth of wonderful places. And I do mean hides. The trick is to get past the tollbooths, the malls, the look-alike suburban developments, and the industrial "parks," and to look a bit deeper. You'd be amazed at what's available out there.

I was.

For instance, while writing "Canoeing the Pinelands," I discovered a wilderness adventure that starts right under a highway viaduct. Doing "Fall Foliage," I found a beautiful boat tour that passes directly beneath the Garden State Parkway. And for "The Cowtown Rodeo," I came upon about a real western rodeo just a few miles from the New Jersey Turnpike.

All of these adventures were news to me. But I hope this book will make these hidden wonders of New Jersey somewhat less hidden.

As I worked on this project and told my friends about it, many reacted with the typical pejorative "Jersey Joke" attitude, saying something along the lines of, "Can you *find* fifty-two things to do in New Jersey?" But my problem was in choosing *only* fifty-two. To paraphrase the old Jimmy Durante line, "I found a million of 'em."

Think about this: the New Jersey Division of Travel and Tourism boasts that the state has 1,056 places listed on the National Historic Register.

Obviously visiting historic places alone would require a lot of weekends.

Still, I'll go on uncovering the state's cache of treasures, and I'd welcome information on additional worthwhile "places to go," "things to do," or "events that happen" in New Jersey. They're out there—just beyond the next exit ramp or behind that shopping mall.

Spring

1 The Shad Festival
Lambertville

A shad is a fish and a bony one at that. About fifteen years ago, the shad had all but stopped their spring run up the Delaware River because the river was a mess. But slowly, persistent conservation efforts began to clear its waters, and gradually the shad returned. In 1981, the village of Lambertville (population 4,000) decided to celebrate the shad's resurgence. The Shad Festival was born. Now, one weekend in late April each year, thousands of people come to Lambertville to shop, to eat, to hear music, to dance, to learn about river ecology, and to watch Fred Lewis.

Fred Lewis?

Fred Lewis is New Jersey's only licensed, commercial, inland fisherman. He lives and works on a minuscule island that sits, oh, maybe fifty feet off the New Jersey side of the river. It's connected to the "mainland" by a rickety, handmade, private footbridge. This island – along with a fishery – has been in the Lewis family for more than 100 years.

Now, six days a week, from mid-March to mid-May, Fred and his crew troll the river for shad with their big net. It takes about six guys to complete the operation, more if the haul is particularly good. The townsfolk purchase the day's catch – if Fred's had any luck. During Shad Festival, Fred performs several

1

trolling demonstrations. Along with about 250 other people, I crossed over to his island to watch him work.

There was no formal announcement, no opening ceremony or gun. Most of us couldn't even tell which one of those guys was Fred. But the crowd lined the riverbank with great anticipation, and when a grizzled-looking man in a bright orange slicker began hauling in a tangle of rope, we figured out two things: one, that was Fred; and two, the fishing had begun. Fred dragged that net about a quarter mile upriver while his helpers sat in a rowboat midstream. Upon reaching an appointed spot, Fred tossed the net into the water. His aides grabbed one side and, with Fred providing on-land resistance, they dragged it slowly downstream toward the concrete and iron bridge to Pennsylvania. As Fred deliberately placed one muddy boot in front of the other, his body angled radically back, someone in the crowd called out to him.

"How's it lookin'?" barked the friendly voice.

"Won't know till I pull 'er in," Fred said without missing a step.

Upon reaching the little island's southern tip, Fred and his helpers hauled in the net. The entire process took about twenty minutes. Fred caught four fish. Just goes to show you–even the pros get skunked.

The news of Fred's poor catch was passed on to the crowd waiting to cross the bridge for the next demonstration, but nobody was deterred. There was a party mood in town.

Indeed, the Shad Festival really amounts to an enormous block party. North Union Street is closed and filled with booths offering everything from shad chowder to fine crafts to silly trinkets to a putt-putt golf fundraiser for the sixth-grade educational fund. Live bands play continuously. The town historical tour runs sporadically. Ten bucks buys a shad dinner. On Saturday night, there's a dance–the Fish Frolic.

But shad hasn't always been Lambertville's claim to fame. The town was an industrial center in the late nineteenth century. The bobby pin was invented here, and wooden wagon wheels, rubber boots, railway cars, locomotives, and bottled beer were made here. Today, the town is filled with fascinating federal and Queen Anne–style houses, narrow tree-lined streets, quaint craft and antique shops, galleries, a bike path that parallels the river and the Delaware & Raritan Canal, cozy bed and breakfasts, and a selection of excellent restaurants. Lambertville remains small-town America. Take Fine's Hardware, for example. It's a living piece of old-style retail Americana with merchandise of every kind – from thumb tacks to washing machines – haphazardly displayed. "Mish-mosh merchandising," my mom would call it.

The shops, too, reflect a grass-roots commerciality. Collectibles, crafts, art, and antiques are displayed in a loving but rough-edged manner that says this is where the craftspeople not only sell, but live, so c'mon in and have a look-see. Places like the Antique Center at the People's Store (a co-op) and the 5 & Dime, which houses an outstanding collection of antique toys, are more fun and fanciful than the typical over-priced high-brow antique shops.

Unlike many of New Jersey's historic districts, Lambertville's buildings span many styles, giving the town a timeless feeling. A small historical museum offers tours and a glimpse into the village's rich past. Take the building at 44 Coryell, now an enchanting bed and breakfast; it was built in three sections, starting before 1800. With a knowledgeable eye, you can track its evolution.

Like Lambertville, the Shad Festival has evolved, too, from a small get-together to one of the state's most popular springtime events. It has been said that if you want to be at the big block party, you should visit the town during festival weekend, but if you want to see the real Lambertville, come around some other time. Luckily, Lambertville's open year-round, so you can do both.

Specifically: For general Lambertville information, call 609-397-0055.

To reach Lambertville: from the north, take US 202 south to the last exit in New Jersey and get on State 29 south. From the south, take the New Jersey Turnpike or I-195 to I-295 north, circumventing Trenton, and exit onto State 29 north.

2 The Pequest Trout Hatchery
Oxford

It's a Saturday in April, about 7:45 A.M. I'm performing my morning run through the local county park. The running path parallels the creek-like Saddle River. I make this run four times a week. I seldom see anyone except other runners and walkers.

But this morning, the riverbanks are lined with dozens of people—mostly men. All are dressed as if they've stepped from the pages of *Field & Stream*, and all hold fishing poles. Not one of them is fishing. They merely stand and wait.

I ponder them as my run takes me along a park access road, past a playground, and then back onto the path and over a footbridge where I see more of them. Some chat idly, one or two smoke, but nobody makes a move toward the water. Why are these folks lined up by the dozens in a place where I had only occasionally seen school kids working five-and-dime rods and reels?

What is going on? That morning's newspaper, which awaits me in my driveway, holds the answer in a small headline in the sports section: "Trout Season Starts Today." At 8:00 A.M. I'd seen them all at 7:45. They'd been anxiously waiting for the "official start."

The fish those anglers sought to snare were all hatched and raised at the Pequest Trout Hatchery in Oxford. The hatchery annually stocks more than 200 New Jersey bodies of water (among them, the Saddle River) with some 600,000 brook, brown, and rainbow trout. Fishing license fees fund the entire process. Because so many of the fish caught in New Jersey's inland waters are given life at the Pequest Trout Hatchery, it's an appropriate place to begin exploring New Jersey freshwater fishing.

In front of the hatchery's visitor's center, a modern, angular building with a facade of glass and variegated, mock-sandstone

5

block, a small fish raceway has been cut into the sidewalk. The group of mixed-species adult trout who live in it greet visitors indifferently, but they illustrate what this place is all about. When we arrived, a handful of boys wearing Cub Scout uniforms were lined up along the raceway, shouting and pointing with fascination. "There's one!" "Look at that one!" "Here's a BIG one!" Mind you, these trout were doing nothing more than slowly lolling from one end of the trough to the other, but to the small boys, just seeing a trout seemed extraordinary enough.

Inside, you learn all about trout. We watched a video that explained the entire spawning process. They're particular creatures, these fish. They need very, very clean water that's just the right temperature, and they want only the best food. Here, they get it. "These fish live in water that's got to be the purest in all of New Jersey," hatchery senior biologist Paul Tarlowe told me.

Out back you see it all in action: the water purification and pumping plant, the long, large raceways, which literally bubble with jumping fish, the nursery, where the baby fish (fry) grow up in special cradling tanks.

But this hatchery is devoted to more than just fish—it attends to all areas of conservation. Back inside, displays show the wildlife that is native to the surrounding area, explain the various branches of the state government that deal with conservation, and afford an opportunity to watch birds. One particularly effective display puts you in charge of creating a computer model that could help preserve and utilize natural lands. Creating public policy is an extremely complicated task, filled with choices that have both benefits and drawbacks. This model illustrates the difficulties—in a stimulating and intriguing way.

The hatchery also offers classes. We attended a session entitled "So, You Want to Take Up Fly Fishing," which reviewed the basics of equipment and fish behavior. Those Cub Scouts were on their way to a session called "Tracks." They were going into the adjacent woods to find and identify various kinds of animal tracks. During the year, the hatchery offers hands-on programs ranging from bird-watching to bow hunting and fly-fishing to spin casting. Almost all of them are free.

One week before trout season opens (late March or early April), the hatchery mounts its annual Open House. The event features a full weekend of family games and activities, as well as an encampment by the New Jersey Muzzle Loading Association, displays by and information from sportsmen's groups, archery and BB shooting ranges, and a chance to meet Smokey the Bear in person.

Set on the Pequest Wildlife Management Area's 1,600 acres, the hatchery offers hiking trails, a picnic area, access to the Pequest River, and a stocked pond where beginners can practice their techniques. ("Remember, we call it fishing," says Tarlowe when asked about his students' success. "We don't call it catching!") With its proximity to the Pequest and Delaware Rivers, the hatchery is a natural jumping-off place for both new and experienced fishermen.

Specifically: The Pequest Trout Hatchery and Natural Resource Education Center (908-637-4125) is located on US 46 in Oxford, about ten miles west of Hackettstown. Hours are: 10:00 A.M. to 4:00 P.M. daily; closed holidays; some evening programs are offered. The hatchery is a good source for fishing site information and regulations. Call for an event schedule, or write to Pequest Trout Hatchery, RR 1, Box 389, Oxford, NJ 07863-9748.

3 Edwin B. Forsythe National Wildlife Reserve
Brigantine

Looking for the Forsythe Refuge just north of Atlantic City, I spotted a sign along US 9 that said "Scott's Landing." It pointed east along an unremarkable road that appeared to go out to sea. In a few miles, another sign pointed to the right. The pavement soon gave way to dirt, and a large sign warned of dire consequences to any who entered the refuge outside the appointed hours – essentially, summer daylight hours.

Immediately, the road became enshrouded by a primeval forest with old, scraggly-looking, and bent trees ensnared by strangling vines and entangled in undergrowth. At the end of the track, in a small clearing, a quartet of pick-up trucks – each attached to a boat trailer and each looking a little the worse for wear – stood like trusty steeds, idly waiting for the return of their masters. The bed of each held various seafaring and fishing items – old netting, bobs, gas cans, and the like.

A small dock stood to the right, abutting a low concrete wall beyond which, in three directions, a sea of swamp grass held itself tall and still in the heavy air. The ocean was not visible here, only various estuaries running to it. Two men stood on the dock, now staring out across the grasses, now fidgeting with lines they had dropped into the water. As I approached, a dark, oblong object scurried across the dirt. It came to rest at the base of the low wall. A crab. Pincers opening and closing nervously, it stood ready for trouble. Five feet away, a large plastic bucket overflowed with his (her?) brothers and sisters.

"These crabs belong to you guys?" I asked the two.

"Yep."

"One's making a getaway," I noted.

"That's okay," the one in the red shirt assured me. "Those are all too small anyway. They're going back."

That's when I noticed the half barrel standing a few yards closer to the water. "Those are the keepers," said the other, a middle-aged fellow in a white baseball cap.

We chatted, these two gentlemen and I. They'd been crabbing since the tide had started climbing up at about ten this morning. It was, they declared, a nice way to kill a day. They dropped a trap dockside and pulled up another that held one keeper out of four. The younger guy held the squirming crustacean carefully between his fingers and showed me how to tell male from female.

"Got a favorite recipe?" I asked.

"Sure," he replied. The recipe involved a careful mix of beer, water, vinegar, red pepper, and several other spices, along with a strong recommendation to soak steamed crabs in the concoction overnight in the refrigerator. "They get tastier that way," he reasoned aloud. "They pick up extra flavor from the shell."

I left them at that point, their bucket overflowing, the older gentleman hustling after a runaway keeper who was trying to scurry back to freedom. Overhead, hundreds of birds flew in great circles, looking for a dinner of their own.

Back on US 9 south I found another sign. This one said, "Forsythe Refuge." Again the road bent sharply, and I found several small buildings and one larger administrative-looking edifice. "Fee Collected Every Day" a sign warned me.

I parked near the small cluster of outbuildings and approached one that promised visitor information. Looking through the front-door glass, it appeared to be nothing more than a wall with a door, like a Hollywood set with only the fronts of buildings. I opened the door and understood why. The far wall, overlooking the vast expanse of swamp, was made of glass. A tabletop-height shelf ran across it. On it rested a registry book, a bird-watching log, and bird-spotting survey forms. Also available were brochures explaining the refuge, a self-guided driving tour, and a list/scorecard of birds to be seen. I took one of each.

About to get back into the car, I noticed the James F. Akers Trail. A sign promised a quarter-mile, self-guided, annotated hiking loop. Walking time required would be one-half to one full hour, depending on my level of interest.

I followed the path. Not ten yards into the woods, I was enveloped by hungry bugs. The bug repellent? In my suitcase at the hotel. I'd have to make this quick. Even walking swiftly, pausing little, and continuously swishing my arms around like a horse's fly-swatting tail, I was able to learn a lot from the trail-side annotations: the difference between black and white oak, that red cedar is really a juniper, that the ubiquitous vines were either Virginia creeper or greenbrier, and that poison ivy runs rampant in this area. Poison ivy? Don't touch, the sign admonished. I didn't.

Safely back in my air-conditioned car, where insects feared to fly, I embarked on the self-guided driving tour. The dry, light-tan dirt road took me through dark and mucky surroundings. My printed guide revealed that the road was constructed from an abandoned railroad bed that once supported tracks to Brigantine Island. Now, the dirt track tops a dike that had been strategically constructed to reclaim this ocean wetlands area and to allow the creatures of the air and water to live naturally. Birds swooped and dove, ascended, and flew off into the distance. An abundance of sandpipers pecked at the sands. A small portion of beach was littered with dead horseshoe crabs. They resembled miniature army tanks that had been stopped in their tracks by an unseen force, and they were now being picked over by ravenous scavengers.

The drive covered eight miles. The printed guide nicely explained how the wetlands reclamation worked, if not much about the animals I saw, but my strongest impression was from the contrast between the quiet wildness of the undisturbed shore and the boisterous, man-made Atlantic City wildness that loomed so close, just down the coast.

Specifically: The Edwin B. Forsythe National Wildlife Refuge (609-652-1665) is open daily throughout the year. It encompasses 39,000 acres. The Brigantine Division is just north of Atlantic City and is the site of the refuge's headquarters and self-guided driving tour; the Barnegat Division is located off US 9 along the western shore of Barnegat Bay; the Holgate Division covers the southern tip of Long Beach Island. A seasonal guide to wildlife activity is available from the park's headquarters. Mailing address: Great Creek Road, PO Box 72, Oceanville, NJ 08231.

4 The New Jersey Wine Trails

Wherever a grape can be grown, man will turn his hand to wine-making. New Jersey is no exception. Seventeen wineries and eight vineyards operate in the state, producing upwards of a quarter of a million gallons of wine annually in more than forty varieties. Here's a look at four of them.

Renault Winery
Egg Harbor City

The Renault Winery can be fascinating, but you have to get past the confused, kitschy architecture first. The overall aim is to create the effect of a Mediterranean villa. Cutesy elements such as exterior staircases and ramps ensconced in mock wine barrels, or tunnel-like interior walkways that seem designed to recall great wine cellars, create a gaudy, Disneyesque effect. It's all a bit much.

But since it has been in operation for 127 years, Renault does have historical interest. An impressive collection of antique wine-making equipment is displayed, and the Champagne Glass Museum—a roomful of champagne glasses collected from every part of the world and every era—showcases its treasures in beautifully worked built-in cabinets beneath a striking Renaissance-style ceiling.

The winery's history is fascinating, and its telling makes the tour worthwhile, but is the wine any good? In the tasting room (decorated like the inside of a wine barrel), I sampled four. The dry whites were nice, but a bit too sweet. The Royal Rouge came across well. Renault is best known for its Blueberry Champagne. It's the sole American champagne of its kind, and it does offer a distinctive taste.

Perhaps the best reason to visit Renault, however, is its food.

On weekend evenings, the winery offers a six-course dinner that has gained a wide reputation for excellence. The Sunday brunch is no less satisfactory. Lunch is served daily at the Garden Cafe. Before your meal, take the tour. The winery's anecdote-rich history is a story well worth hearing.

Tamuzza Vineyards
Hope
Entering the Tamuzza property, you'll turn onto a dirt road that heads uphill beside the vineyard. Ahead, atop the hill, rises an overwhelming nouveau Italianate/Mediterranean villa-style home; the effect could not be more dramatic. That, however, is not the winery. That's the Tamuzza homestead. Halfway up the hill, the road sends you sharply to your right, across the vine fields, and then to your left again, until you arrive at a tiny building that seems like a misplaced roadside stand. This is the "winery," or at least the reception and retail store area. Step inside.

Paul Tamuzza, proprietor and master vintner, was absent the day I visited, and no winery tours were being conducted. "Tours are usually given on weekends," a cheerful young lady named Rachel told me, as if this weren't a Saturday. "But even so, it's best to call ahead." Too bad. Mr. Tamuzza, word has it, is very knowledgeable—and voluble—when it comes to his wines.

Unable to tour, I tasted. More significantly, I bought. Being partial to whites, I discovered that Tamuzza produces some good ones, especially its Seyval Blanc, which I took home for only $6.75. Like Renault, with its blueberry champagne and sweet rosés, Tamuzza's strength is in its sweet offerings, specifically, a singular Almondique, a white variety flavored with natural almond that does very well as a dessert wine.

Tamuzza offers no "shtick," but the wine's good. And that's good enough for me.

Four Sisters Winery
Belvidere

Four Sisters Winery at Matarazzo Farms specializes in festivals. With everything from "Hike the Hills Day" to celebrations of strawberries, wines in spring, peaches, bluegrass music, the fall harvest, and wines in fall, as well as a cross-country skiing get-together in mid-winter and two Native American Powwows, this enterprise has become a major northwestern New Jersey tourist attraction. What's more, they have a great bakery.

I have to confess that I didn't do any wine tasting at Four Sisters. I'd just come from Tamuzza, and I'd had my fill, but the Matarazzo family's wines have won a number of awards. Reliable word-of-mouth promises that the wines produced here are palate-worthy. You can sample the wines in a small, pleasant building attached to the farm store. Professional art and photography grace the walls, and there are terrific views of the surrounding fields, vineyards, and hills through the large windows and from the adjacent deck.

In addition to the standard winery tour, the staff explores and explains the vineyards and also regularly gives special classes.

The winery's strength resides in its appeal as a family-centered event specialist. If you've got kids, and you want to keep them happy while you do your wine tasting, visit during any of the farm's festivals. There's always something going on: music, storytelling, hayrides, hay bale mazes, grape stomping, dancing – you name it. You can even pick your own veggies and pumpkins in season.

Cream Ridge Winery
Cream Ridge

You've got to like Tom Amabile. He likes what he does, and his enthusiasm is infectious. A former systems specialist for Public

Service Electric & Gas, Tom has allowed a kitchen hobby to sweep him into an entirely new second career–master vintner. You've got to like Cream Ridge Winery, too. Set up in a large, barn-like structure, it's designed as if Tom and his wife Joan simply let the business grow out of the family kitchen like a runaway vine. In the front parlor-like room, you find a pleasant gift and wine shop. Behind, in an oversized garage, you find the winery. One side of the garage has a balcony, where wine tour participants gather while Tom stands by his machinery and explains what he does.

What Tom does is create some unique fruit wines. The man is clearly a born tinkerer, and he loves to tinker with fruits to see how he can develop them into wine. His cherry and cranberry wines recently won gold medals at the New Jersey Wine Competition. ("Only three golds were given out," he's quick to note.) But, it's the Cream Ridge Black Raspberry that leaves people talking. Why? It's dry. Tom uses a cold fermentation process, but the unique dryness is derived from oak barrel aging. ("Aging fruit wines in oak is unique," he says. "Not too many folks do that.") The results are hard to describe. Best to head on over to Cream Ridge and sample a bottle.

Specifically: The New Jersey Department of Agriculture/ New Jersey Wine Industry Advisory Council publishes a guide to the New Jersey Wine Trail. Call 609-292-8853 to obtain a copy.

To reach Renault Winery (609-965-2111), take the Garden State Parkway to Exit 44, make a sharp right onto Moss Mill Road (County Alternate 561), go five miles to Bremen Avenue, turn right and go another quarter mile.

Tamuzza Vineyards (908-459-5878) is reached from I-80 Exit 12. Go south into Hope and turn right at the blinking light, go two blocks and turn right onto Mt. Herman Road (County

655 north), go 1.5 miles, take a left on Locust Lake Road, continue for one mile, and then take a right on Cemetery Road. Turn left at the stone columns 500 feet later.

Four Sisters Winery at Matarazzo Farms (908-475-3671) is on County 519. From I-80, take Exit 12, turn left at the bottom of the ramp and go 6.5 miles. From I-78, take State 31 north until it ends, turn left on US 46, pass one light, then turn right onto County 519, and continue for two miles.

Cream Ridge Winery (609-259-9797) is located on County 539 near Allentown (see Chapter 27). Take Exit 7-A from the New Jersey Turnpike to I-195 east, take Exit 8, and then follow County 539 south for three miles.

5 Laughing All the Way
Ocean City

You've got to love a resort town that has a sense of humor. Like a shore town that stages an annual Miss Crustacean Beauty Pageant, complete with a miniature mollusk-sized runway surrounded by all the traditional pomp and circumstance normally reserved for human beauties. Or a resort that produces an annual Pun-Off in which the person who provokes the loudest groans and worst facial cringes from the audience wins. Or a resort that annually celebrates Hermit Crab Day, in which a character named Martin T. Mollusk, described in a news release as "a testy hermit crab addicted to stale pizza crust and rancid swamp water," appears on the beach in search of his shadow. Should he see it, so it is told, summer comes one week early that year. It is no coincidence that in nearly twenty years of this riotous ritual, Martin has never failed to see his shadow.

What can you say about a seaside resort that can see beyond the sun, sand, salt, and water to provide some silliness? You've gotta love Ocean City.

Ocean City stages funny and fun special events almost all year-round. Weekly happenings begin with the town's own Easter parade, run right through the early October Indian Summer Weekend, and keep going till New Year's eve, with the shore's biggest First Night celebration (see Chapter 51). In June the action moves into high gear, and throughout the summer a special contest, celebration, or parade of some kind takes place almost daily. The events are good old-fashioned, wholesome, clean fun, aimed at families. Few seaside resorts cater better to mom, dad, and the kids. Why? Because Ocean City's family roots run deep.

Ocean City was founded in the 1870s by the three Lake brothers—Methodist ministers all—who were dedicated to the notion that evils such as gambling and drinking had no place where families gathered. In 1879 they signed a covenant banning such vices from the town. Today, the town remains liquor-free and devoid of games of chance.

Walk Ocean City's boardwalk and you'll find enough shops selling T-shirts, saltwater taffy, used books, and swimwear to supply yourself with these items for a lifetime. But unlike the more carnival-like boardwalks of Wildwood, Atlantic City, Asbury Park, and Seaside Heights, you won't be harangued by hawkers trying to entice you to "take a chance" at this game or that. Yes, there are video games to be played, and there's a small child-friendly amusement arcade at the boardwalk's north end. But you'll find a low-key atmosphere, a live-and-let-live feeling, and you'll discover the Music Pier.

The Music Pier takes you back to the 1930s, the time of marathon dance contests. The town recently gave its marvel of period architecture a $4 million renovation, but you still sit on folding chairs. Many gatherings there, like the Artisans Band Concert or the Youth On Stage performances, induce smiles with their thoroughly homemade quality. Professional concerts are staged as well. Indeed, the Ocean City Pops is the shore's only resident professional ensemble and plays everything from Sousa to Victor Herbert to Beethoven. At times the group also accompanies special performances, like a fully mounted production of *South Pacific* or presentations by the New Jersey Ballet.

Other unique Ocean City items of note: the town has its own nine-hole golf course, supports a small airport, and offers shopping in a true "downtown" environment. Remember, nearly 20,000 people call Ocean City home full time. It's a real place, not just a tourist trap, so you can wander along Asbury Avenue and find a plethora of fine shops supplying not-so-touristy items such as Oriental rugs, antiques, and furniture. You'll also find a series of small, storefront restaurants with good fare at reasonable prices where you'll feel comfortable with your toddler, your teenager, or your date.

Downtown is home to the Discovery Sea Shell Museum, a collection of more than 10,000 shells, including the famous, one-of-a-kind, Siamese twin-helmet shell.

Ocean City's spirit, however, is best captured by its dedication to crabby special events – the Miss Crustacean Beauty Pageant, Hermit Crab Day, and its World Championship Hermit Crab Races. To capture that spirit, let me finish with a descriptive quote from an obscure tome entitled "The Martin Z. Mollusk Story (Rhyme & Punishment)":

... Miss Crustacean, USA
The pageant where a vast array

Of lovely shellfish meet to vie
For Queen of Crabdom, how they try
To bump and grind in gaudy dress
To smile and otherwise impress

The judges on the pristine sand
Of Ocean City, that's a grand
Resort upon the Jersey shore. . .
This pageant siphons crabs galore

From every state where crabs exist,
From every cove where crabs persist
In doting over daughters whom
"Look beautiful," I presume

Are beautiful, at least to fish. . .
They come in droves, it is their wish,
Nay, more than that, it is their duty
To be proclaimed "Crustacea's Beauty. . ."

The poetic history goes on like this for many chapters, but you get the point. Folks in Ocean City know how to laugh.

Specifically: Ocean City is located south of Atlantic City. From the Garden State Parkway southbound, take Exit 30; northbound travelers use Exit 25. Ocean City lodging runs the full range, from bed and breakfasts to full-service resort hotels. For general information, brochures, and event schedules, call 1-800-232-2465.

6 Biking the Back Roads

"In a car, you're always in a compartment, and because you're used to it you don't realize that through that car window everything you see is just more TV. You're a passive observer and it is all moving by you boringly in a frame.

"On a cycle the frame is gone. You're completely in contact with it all. You're *in* the scene, not just watching it anymore, and the sense of presence is overwhelming."

—Robert M. Pirsig
Zen and the Art of Motorcycle Maintenance

Pirsig was talking about the joys of driving a motorcycle. But he just as easily could have been talking about pedaling a bicycle. Indeed, if anything, his observations are even more true on a bike because you're not only in the scene, you're in it under your own power. Biking affords contemplative possibilities simply not available at greater speeds.

Any cycling enthusiast should take the time to visit the U.S. Bicycling Hall of Fame in Somerville. The collection of antique bikes and biking paraphernalia is fascinating and, if you can be in the area during Memorial Day weekend, you can take in the oldest continuously operating major bike race in the country, the Tour of Somerville.

If you're a doer rather than a watcher, New Jersey affords a surprising variety of biking terrains. Hilly rides, flat rides, waterside rides, and urban rides are all possible here. The state Department of Transportation prints pamphlets describing nine individual rides that, together, cover most of the state. The following is a glimpse at two of those rides, plus another ride of my own fancy.

Round Valley Roundabout

Tucked just off to the south of busy I-78 and US 22, Round Valley Reservoir is the centerpiece of Round Valley State Recreation Area, a popular weekend getaway spot. You can begin this 28.5-mile ride at the Recreation Area, or start at the East Whitehouse fire station in the small town of Whitehouse, just south of US 22. The overall circuit covers moderately hilly terrain and, since it sticks largely to back roads, only a few spots are busy with auto traffic.

Along the way you'll pass through Oldwick, a tiny town founded circa 1740, that boasts a number of fine antique shops and an old-fashioned general store. When you arrive in Mountainville, you can stop in at the Kitchen Caboodle for a gourmet box-style lunch. Want to add a continental touch to that box-lunch picnic? Detour to Saw Mill Road in Mountainville and visit the Tewksbury Wine Cellars.

For those who start in Whitehouse, several miles after leaving Mountainville, you'll pass under I-70 and US 22 and then skirt the Round Valley Recreation Area. It's a good spot for a picnic or a swim, but be cautious of traffic on weekends. Continuing south, the route heads toward the microscopic town of Stanton. Before you get to the village, however, a turn onto County 618 can lead you into the Hunterdon County Arboretum, a converted commercial nursery in which a variety of trees are grouped into single-species groves. In Stanton, another classic country general store provides an opportunity to stop for food or drink.

Battle of Monmouth Ride

Monmouth Battlefield State Park marks the site of the longest battle of the American Revolution. It's also the start of this twenty-eight-mile loop through rolling countryside that passes a full range of New Jersey scenery—horse farms, suburban tracts, orchards, and woodlands. The route not only explores the battlefield, but it also goes to Holmdel County Park, home to yet another garden, the Holmdel Arboretum. The twenty-acre arboretum contains nearly 500 species of plants. Pick up a plant index as you enter and see how many you can identify.

In Freehold, a stop at the Monmouth County Historical Society on Court Street will give you an overview of the area's significant role in U.S. history.

A Deep Southern Excursion
I discovered this route while exploring the so-called Delsea region. The roads are good, traffic is light, the going is fairly flat, and the environment has a subtropical flavor. If you're riding in the heart of summertime, be sure to carry water, bug repellent, and sun block.

Start in Mauricetown (pronounced Morris-town), a small village at a crook in the Maurice (pronounced Morris) River. Riding out of town on Haleyville Road, take a left onto State 47 for a few hundred yards. Then go right onto County 670 (also marked as Alternate 47), which will take you to the edge of Belleplain State Forest. Follow County 550-Spur south (Delmont-Belleplain Road). When County 550-Spur turns right, continue straight ahead into Delmont. Hook up with State 47 there, take a right, go a mile or two, then go left on Grade Road (County 616), which will take you into Heiserville. Follow County 616 (Heiserville Road) as it winds north and parallels the Maurice River. It will pass through Leesburg and then into Dorchester. Both towns sit right on the river and make good spots for a scenic riverside break. North of Dorchester, County 616 will take you back to State 47. Go left, then right back onto County 670 (Haleyville Road), and you'll return to Mauricetown.

Throughout the region, farmlands mix with densely over-grown areas of woodlands and jungle-like undergrowth, com-bined with marshes that characterize the Delaware Bay and the silica-rich sandy soils that fostered the region's great glassmak-ing industries. You'll not find anything like it anywhere else in New Jersey.

Specifically: The New Jersey Department of Transportation (609-530-8062) offers an array of literature on biking in the state, including nine brochures detailing bike tour routes of varying types. Write to Bicycle Advocate, NJDOT, 1035 Parkway Avenue, CN 600, Trenton, NJ 08625. Be sure to ask for the pamphlet, "New Jersey Bicycling Information," which covers a range of resources, including a bibliography of touring books that cover the state.

A number of good books can be found at the library or bookstores that outline a variety of rides in the state.

7 A Deep-Sea Fish Story

The *Doris Mae IV*, owned and operated by the brothers Eble, sets sail three times daily out of Barnegat Light. Mornings are for half-day fluke fishing. At four in the afternoon, it takes an hour-long family cruise. Hard-core anglers come aboard at 7:00 P.M. for the night bluefish run. This is a boat that, clearly, never rests.

Doris Mae's patrons—like most other party fishing boat patrons—come aboard because they love to fish. But unfortunately, I've always been too easily victimized by dizziness and vertigo to enjoy fishing by boat. This trip was no exception.

The anglers began to gather at the dock two hours before sailing time. They waited by their automobiles, sipping beer and soda and picnicking in the parking lot.

"Why," I asked my friend Bob, "are they here so early?"

"They want to be sure they get the good spot on the boat," he told me.

Some, it seems, believe that good luck comes only from fishing the boat's stern. Others insist on a place along the bow. You claim a spot by setting your pole into one of the holders along the main deck's rail. Then you wait.

The ride out to sea took about an hour; sometimes it runs an hour and a half, depending on where the fish are purported to be. Captain Ron Eble, equipped with the best sonar fish-spotting equipment (which can even differentiate among fish species) and the best rumor-sorting ear (which can even determine which fish reports from other boats are meaningful) sailed to a predetermined spot.

On deck, some customers stared at the dark waters or peered into the night. Others rode inside, eating hot dogs and burgers grilled by a deckhand or food from their own coolers. Folks chatted or watched a large TV screen as they waited.

Suddenly, the ceaseless rumble of the dual diesel engines

25

changed cadence, a bell rang, and, like alerted firefighters, everyone took a post. The fishing began.

I didn't fish. I didn't even attempt to stand up, but I did
watch and listen. The people were quiet. Quiet like that, I
quickly learned, means bad fishing. After a while, the bell rang
again, the engines started, and we steamed farther into the night.

At stop number two, infrequent and sporadic shouts were
heard. "I got one!" "Whoa!" "Hey! That guy got a shark."

The less successful among us drifted indoors to crack open
a beer, eat another hoagie, and bemoan their fishing fate. "I'm
just out here on a thirty-five-dollar boat ride," complained one.
"Did you see that guy next to me?" another asked rhetorically.
"He's pulling them in left and right. Left and right. And me, I got
exactly nothing!"

"It's the green light," another luckless one stated unequivo-
cally. "All the guys who are landing fish got those green lights."
The mysterious green light affixes to the end of the rod and is
reputed to attract fish, although no one can say exactly how
or why.

"See that guy?" said the luckless, green lightless one, pointing out the window. "He's getting 'em like crazy. I'm going to
check it out. I give you ten-to-one he got the green light."

A moment passed. The boat rolled with a wave. My stomach
waved with the roll. The disgruntled angler returned.

"No light!" he proclaimed joyously. "No light! There's hope!
We better get back out there!"

Nearby a young woman slept. "I'm the designated driver,"
she told Bob. "We have a two-hour drive when we get back, so I
sleep on the boat."

The bell rang. The boat moved. Thank goodness, I thought,
we're going in.

But, no. The engines fired back, the bell rang still again. And
everyone's luck changed.

A great catch of blues

A constant refrain of "I got one!" now emanated from the deck. Although fully out of earshot from the complaints of thirty-five-dollar boat rides, Ron had obviously been aware that his customers had not been having much luck that night. With a professional's smarts he brought them to a large school of bluefish. We stayed there for an hour. By the time we docked, the clock said 4:30 A.M., although we had been scheduled to return at about two. These folks had come to catch fish, and the captain worked the extra hours to make them happy.

All the passengers ate fresh bluefish that night. Except me. I had some thick pink liquid with some crunchy white pills, and was just thankful that the earth had stopped rocking under my feet.

Specifically: The *Doris Mae IV* sails daily; call 908-494-2369 for information.

The New Jersey Division of Travel and Tourism's Outdoor Guide lists nearly 200 boat basins and marinas, most of which will either offer party or charter fishing boats, or can refer you to the nearest facility that does. Call 1-800-537-7397 for a copy of the guide.

8 Hiking

The Appalachian Trail, possibly the single best-known hiking trail on the continent, rambles some 2,000 miles from Georgia to Maine. The trail enters New Jersey at the Delaware Water Gap and follows the Kittatiny Ridge for more than forty miles to High Point. There, the trail moves sharply east and crosses through the heart of Waywayanda State Park and Hewitt State Forest. When it approaches Greenwood Lake, it veers to the north and disappears into New York.

You can hop on the trail at any number of places for short hikes of varying degrees of difficulty. Anywhere you join it, the trail is marked by its signature white blazes.

Casual walkers should remember that, while the mountains of New Jersey may not be regarded with the same awe as those of New England, this is still hill country, and in many places the traveling involves fairly strenuous uphill and downhill scrambles.

The Kittatiny Ridge

The walk along the Kittatiny Ridge, from the northern side of the Delaware Water Gap National Recreation Area to the southern terminus of Stokes State Forest, offers wonderful views of horse and farm country to the east and fine glimpses of the Delaware Valley to the west. Winter hikers with sharp eyes – or a good pair of binoculars – might well spot bald eagles perched high in the trees overlooking the river.

Parking is available adjacent to the Appalachian Trail just south of Millbrook Village along County 602, and also a bit more than four miles north, where County 627 intersects the trail. If you're looking for a longer trek, arrange a pick-up at

Culver's Gap in Stokes State Forest, about twelve miles north. Walking north, the eastern highland vista is pockmarked by small lakes – Farview, Swarstwood, Plymouth, and Owassa to name a few – that enhance the views. A side trip into Millbrook Village, a re-created nineteenth-century community, adds another kind of texture to the trek.

Waywayanda
Waywayanda State Park offers a wealth of hiking and history. Approximately 2.5 miles south of the Appalachian Trail lies Lake Waywayanda, where you'll find the remains of a charcoal blast furnace that produced iron to make shovels and swords during the Civil War. An abandoned iron mine can be found near the junction of the Appalachian Trail and the trail south to the lake. In the eastern section of the park, the trail touches upon and intersects with other trails that penetrate a dense hemlock forest, a veritable untamed jungle that is quite unique to the region. Still farther east is a cedar swamp thick with tall white cedars and showy rhododendron more often found in coastal marshlands.

SOUTH

The Batona Trail
The name Batona is an acronym for Back To Nature, the name adopted in the 1960s by the Philadelphia hiking club that created this pathway through the heart of southern New Jersey's Pine Barrens. Today, it's still the longest blazed trail in the area. In contrast to the more alpine nature of the Appalachian Trail, Batona wends its way through lowland wilderness dense with wild berries (huckle, blue, winter, and choke), orchids, and

some 100 other species of herbaceous plants. Just watch out for the thick colonies of poison sumac and poison ivy.

Here, too, you'll find the cedar swamps. The abundant cedar trees are what first attracted European settlers to the region. The trail also winds through an area known as The Pine-Plains, a fascinating tract of stunted forest filled with scrub oak and pitch pine that grow, for reasons that remain unknown, to a maximum height of about twelve feet and an average of about four feet.

The Pine Barrens, of course, are anything but barren. The name originally indicated that the wet, sandy soils were not conducive to raising the traditional crops that European settlers wanted to grow, not that the land had no commercial value.

Along the Batona Trail you'll discover the remnants of several settlements, the most prominent of which is Batsto Village in Wharton State Forest. Batsto functioned first as a bog iron and glassmaking center, and later, under the ownership of Joseph Wharton, as a gentleman's farm. This 100,000-acre tract sits atop one of the continent's largest subterranean water supplies, the Cohansey Aquifer, estimated to hold some 17 trillion gallons. Wharton conceived of the aquifer as a gargantuan underground reservoir. His plan was to dam the main streams and rivers and sell water to the nearby cities, especially Philadelphia. Luckily for us, he was thwarted by politics.

The Batona Trail continues north from Batsto – just follow the pink blazes. Its path crosses a great number of local and county roads, which makes it easy to access the trail for shorter out-and-back hikes. Its northern/western terminus is at Ong's Hat in Lebanon State Forest. Camping, swimming, and other recreations can be pursued in these state parks and forests, and the old sand roads make for excellent mountain biking.

The combination of the sandy soil and the abundant water

create the area's essential swampy character—an environment bugs love. Be sure to carry plenty of bug repellent spray.

Specifically: The New Jersey Division of Travel and Tourism's Outdoor Guide lists many parks with hiking trails; call 1-800-537-7397 for a copy.

The Appalachian Trail

For information on the trail in New Jersey parks, call the Delaware Water Gap National Recreation Area, 908-496-4458 or 717-588-2435; Stokes State Forest, 201-948-3820; High Point State Park, 201-875-4800; or Waywayanda State Park, 201-853-4462.

The Batona Trail

Call Bass River State Forest, 609-296-1114; Lebanon State Forest, 609-726-1191; or Wharton State Forest, 908-561-0024.

Special Needs?

A number of parks around the state offer hiking/walking trails for people with disabilities. Among them are: the Braille Trail at the Frelinghuysen Arboretum in Morristown (201-326-7600); Cattus Island Park in Toms River (908-270-6960), and the Trailside Discovery Trail at Watchung Reservation in Mountainside (908-789-3670). The New Jersey Division of Travel and Tourism's Outdoor Guide lists several others; call 1-800-537-7397 for a copy.

9 The New Jersey Film Festival
New Brunswick

Some of the titles you know. Many you've never heard of. Many are somewhere between – well recognized (if not revered) by film buffs, but only a vague imprint on the general public's consciousness. There are familiar titles such as Alfred Hitchcock's *Dial M for Murder,* more esoteric titles like Louis Bunuel's *L'Age d'Or,* and unheard-of titles like David Russell's *Spanking the Monkey.*

No matter if you've heard of the film, or even seen it before, New Brunswick's New Jersey Film Festival offers nonstop cinematic food for thought.

New Brunswick is home to the main campus of Rutgers University, and the film festival is the creation of Albert Nigrin, a lecturer in the Rutgers Film Studies program and director of the Rutgers Film Co-op. In the early 1980s, fresh out of graduate school, Nigrin put up $300 to start the festival's reels rolling. "We showed films on a pull-down screen in the grad students' commuter lounge," says Nigrin. "It was a free festival, but it was pretty rough around the edges."

Today, Nigrin directs a program that, during its last spring installment, featured some seventy-five films and thirty-one other events, such as filmmaking workshops. The program also stages summer and fall installments. (Be aware that these seasons relate to the university's academic calendar, so the spring series begins in late January and runs through late April.)

Featured on the spring schedule is the United States Super-8 Film & Video Festival – the only juried showcase for Super-8 millimeter films in North America. You remember Super-8. You, your mom and dad, or maybe even your grandparents made home movies using it. While Super-8 has been surpassed by camcorder/video technology, young filmmakers find it a fertile format for experimentation and artistic expression, which explains why the Rutgers Film Co-op has no trouble finding entries. Up to 130 films, ranging in length from a few minutes to half an hour, are received each year from around the U.S. and Canada. They are screened and judged in February and provide some extremely vivid imagery, social commentary, and, yes, even laughs.

The film festival is driven by a multifaceted philosophy. "We want to educate and enlighten the community about media arts," notes Nigrin. "Our main mission is to be artistically minded in our curating. We think of motion pictures as something to stimulate the brain, so we provide free program notes, with cast listings, background, and some form of criticism. Many of the films haven't made it to the area or didn't get a long enough commercial run."

Another goal is "to serve under-served audiences," Nigrin emphasizes. The presentation of such series as "Looking Out: A Gay and Lesbian Festival" and "Women's Works," and collections focusing on African American, Asian American, Native American, and Latino themes bespeaks that purpose. "We're trying to build a film culture in the area. The first step is showing good films," he points out.

The screenings aren't always serious. A recent Halloween 3-D Festival featured 1950s horror films like *Revenge of the Creature*. The evening devoted to the annual Thomas Edison Black Maria Film & Video Festival Touring Program presents highlights from the year's best experimental films.

Screenings take place Friday and Saturday nights at the university's Milledoler Hall. On Sunday evenings, movies run at the State Theater, an archetypal Art Deco movie house that seats more than 1,800. Nigrin is especially pleased to show classic big-screen movies in such a classic setting. "It gives the audience an opportunity to see films in the proper surroundings, in all their wide-screen splendor," he says.

Guest lecture appearances by directors such as Martin

Scorcese (*Taxi Driver, GoodFellas*, etc.) and Paul Morrisey (who directed the Andy Warhol films) illustrate just how this film festival has grown, and how seriously it is regarded by filmmakers. But Nigrin has plans to develop this event even further. Within a few years, he hopes to have created the New Jersey International Film Festival—a one-week series of New Jersey premieres and revivals that would constitute an event on a par with the New York Film Festival and Utah's Sundance Festival. A "start-up version" is expected to begin in summer 1996.

Festival-goers also can take advantage of New Brunswick's other offerings. Catch a matinee at the George Street Playhouse or the Crossroads Theater Company, two groups that have a reputation for excellence and for developing new, high-quality plays; the Crossroads has gained national prominence among African American theater groups.

Or visit one of Rutgers' three excellent museums. The Jane Voorhees Zimmerli Art Museum holds a permanent collection of eighteenth- and nineteenth-century works and offers changing exhibitions. The museum's printmaking exhibit earns high accolades. The Geology Museum displays artifacts, fossils, minerals, etc., and the New Jersey Museum of Agriculture (on the adjacent Cook College campus) explores all facets of the agricultural sciences. Of special note are the museum's photograph collection and its historical agriculture exhibits.

Of course, Rutgers and New Brunswick offer many forms of entertainment, from sports to the performing arts, but it is somehow fitting that New Jersey's state university is gaining recognition for its film festival. After all, the movies were invented in New Jersey.

Specifically: New Brunswick can be reached from Exit 9 of the New Jersey Turnpike, or by taking US 1 to State 18 north.

For New Jersey Film Festival screening and workshop schedules and admission fees, or for Rutgers Film Co-op membership information, call 908-932-8482.

Call for the production schedules of the George Street Playhouse (908-846-2895) and the Crossroads Theater Company (908- 249-5560).

For museum hours and information, call: Jane Voorhees Zimmerli Art Museum (908-932-7237); Rutgers Geology Museum (908-932-7243); New Jersey Museum of Agriculture (908-249-2077).

10 Not Just Gambling (You Can Bet on It)
Atlantic City

Atlantic City has long reigned as an American vacation icon. Many elements that symbolize a shore visit were first conceived here. The boardwalk, for example, was first constructed in 1870 to provide a place to walk easily by the sea and to shop, eat, and be merry. So merry, in fact, that the boardwalk was soon extended out over the water, and the amusement pier was invented. The year was 1882, and Atlantic City's heyday had begun.

The good times lasted well into the 1950s. But by the mid-1960s "AC" had badly deteriorated from the Queen Resort to an ageing matriarch. Then the casinos came.

Today tourists make more than thirty million visits to Atlantic City. The vast majority come to play the slots, shuffle the cards, roll the dice, or spin the roulette wheel. The boardwalk bustles. The night sky blazes with neon fire. There are those who condemn Atlantic City's casino-fed rebirth, but it has brought new life to the city. An excitement that runs along the four-mile boardwalk spills over onto Atlantic and Pacific Avenues.

I'm not a gamer—a "player" as they say—so I'll not attempt to differentiate among the grand casinos. I'm sure that regular visitors can discern the nuances that separate Trump's Castle from Trump Plaza, or Bally's World from TropWorld. I'm also sure that folks have their personal favorites, just as I, an avid skier, have my favorites among ski resorts. But I will say that the action moves nonstop, and with newly approved twenty-four-hour gambling, there's never a time when the slot machine bells aren't tingling or the croupiers dealing. If you're attracted to this kind of action, you'll find a happy home here.

If you're not a gamer, what can you do in Atlantic City? Well for one thing, you can eat very, very well. Most of the casinos offer sumptuous and lavish buffet spreads for extremely reasonable prices. Each casino provides about a half dozen restaurants, and the culinary styles span the world, from Chinese food to Japanese and French. Outside the casino hotels, places like Abe's Oyster House and Dock's Oyster House, both on Atlantic Avenue, carry on the city's longstanding tradition of purveying superb local seafood.

World-class entertainment, too, can keep the nongambler happy. In the casinos' "big rooms" and "lounges," you find names like Bill Cosby, Frank Sinatra–well, you name it. Or if you like lavish musical productions, Atlantic City's stage shows can match the Las Vegas reviews any day.

The entertainment goes beyond gaming houses, highlighted by a number of annual festivals and events. The Miss America Pageant, of course, remains the city's single best-known happening. Again, enjoyment is a matter of taste; ardent feminists and their sympathizers will find no joy in the pageant, but the collection of pretty young women, the pressure of chasing some ambiguous championship, and the ongoing highjinks add nicely to the city's mindless frolic. Little known to most familiar only with the televised finals: almost all the preliminary events before the finals are offered for free or for a minimal ticket fee. One example is the "Show Me Your Shoes" parade, in which the contestants glide down the boardwalk on floats and in cars, lifting a leg high when spectators shout "Show us your shoes!" It's a traditional favorite.

Come spring, the town mounts a seafood festival that attracts thousands. In the fall, the world's largest antiques fair is staged in the Convention Hall, featuring nearly 7,000 exhibitors. Anyone with even the mildest affection for antiques will find something to marvel about. In February, antique cars fill the bill on an equally grand scale.

Indeed, the Convention Hall itself is worthy of a visit. Built

Lucy, the Margate elephant, is six stories high

in 1929, it was then the world's largest auditorium constructed without interior posts. Recently renovated, the main auditorium can seat some 22,000 people, and the main exhibition space spans 300,000 square feet under a 137-foot arched roof. Collegiate football was once played in here.

You can play golf nearby (see Chapter 17), or fish from the beach or from a boat, and if the honky-tonk bustle becomes overbearing, you can find peace and quiet at the Forsythe Wildlife Preserve (see Chapter 3).

Kids are not forgotten in Atlantic City. Classic roller coasters and other rides and amusements are found at TropWorld's Tivoli Pier and the Central Pier on the boardwalk. And a visit to the gigantic Lucy the Elephant in Margate, located just south of AC, is one of the New Jersey shore's longstanding traditions. No kid ever looked at the six-story-high Lucy without dropping his or her jaw.

Atlantic City is not everybody's cup of tea. In 1942, in the first act of his Pulitzer Prize–winning play, *The Skin of Our Teeth,* Thornton Wilder chose to use this "playground by the sea" to represent man's self-indulgent, decadent state just prior to the biblical Flood. The city's popularity, however, goes well beyond the fast-paced, glitzy casino ambience. From simple sunbathing on the pure white beach sands or a slow ride in a boardwalk roller chair to an excellent meal or a humongous antique show, the area offers much more than gaming.

Specifically: For general information, call the Convention and Visitors Bureau at 609-348-7130 or 1-800-262-7395.

To reach Atlantic City, take the Garden State Parkway to the Atlantic City Expressway. The city is served by Amtrak trains, and a variety of day bus trips run from all over the region; the airport is served by USAir, United Express, Northwest Airlink, and other regional carriers.

11 Playing on the Delaware River

The Delaware Water Gap National Recreation Area
The Delaware River runs 390 miles from north-central New York state to the Delaware Bay. Its most visually striking section is a New Jersey treasure – the Delaware Water Gap. At the Gap, the river cuts through the side of Kittatinny Mountain, whose rocks make up the highest ridge of all the Appalachians from New York to Tennessee.

We walked along the river for 1.5 miles on an old railroad bed now called the Karamac Road Trail. Several well-worn, but sometimes steep detours ran down to the water. That's where the kids found the abandoned bridge abutments. For them, finding the stone and concrete slabs, overgrown with grasses and vines, was like discovering an ancient Roman ruin, complete with hieroglyphic graffiti dating to 1979. It was a perfect place to throw stones or cast sticks into the river and watch them float away.

We drove north on Old Mine Road, a bumpy affair, and noticed that the water's edge was lined with people fishing. We stopped at the Copper Mine Trail trailhead. I parked next to the port-o-potty, but nobody had to go. Good thing. "There's a tarantula in there!" we were warned by a small boy dressed in a Ninja Turtle raincoat. "Don't go in!"

Of course, Dan and his pal Aaron immediately opened the port-o-potty door. There it was! Well, if it wasn't a tarantula, at least it was a gnarly-looking, extremely large, black spider. We left him alone and went to search for the abandoned copper mines that give the trail its name.

The Copper Mine Trail runs up to the Appalachian Trail along Kittatiny Ridge, but the old mines are no more than a quarter mile up a side track. What a beautiful side track. The earth practically gleamed red, and a stream bounced energetically

down the steep hillside, cascading over several small waterfalls
and pooling where the slope formed shelves. We reached a mine
and found the entrance boarded up neatly with heavy lumber.
A small doorway was set in the middle.

"Don't open it!" the kids cried.

I opened it. Nothing to see but – dark.

Aaron clambered up the trail beyond the mine. The path
ascended steeply next to tumbling water, over moss-slickened
rocks and tree roots. I followed. A crumbling concrete dam
pooled the water about a hundred feet above the mine. Above
that, a larger cascade glinted like flowing diamonds in the sun.
We reached a ledge and looked back. A narrow corridor of dense
forest was cut by the beautifully singing stream. Aaron wanted
to continue up the steep ledge, but I glumly informed him we
were out of time.

On the way back, the boys set a block of wood afloat in the
stream.

"Where do you think our wood block is now?" Dan wondered when we were about halfway home.

"Imagine it floated to the ocean and washed up at the beach
when we were there in the summer?" Aaron replied.

"It probably floated to Philadelphia and got pulled onto a
ship bound for the Orient," I declared.

"Cool," they said in an awed whisper.

Tubing

If a wood block could float the Delaware, so could we. After all,
we've rafted the icy waters and Class 3 rapids of Maine's Kenne-
bec and Colorado's Turner Rivers. So, really now, was this *floating* going to challenge us? Was this going to frighten us with
excitement? I didn't think so.

The twelve-year-old girls who were my companions tried
their best to make it otherwise, however. Laina's friend, Nancy,

adeptly worked herself into a nervous state. "I'm so scared. I'm so scared. I'm so scared," she repeated like a frenzy-inducing mantra. Laina, who had paddled dauntlessly when the whirling Maine waters had whipped our raft about like a toy tug in a torrent, caught the fever and began professing terror of the Delaware's lazy flow.

"Just hold the tube behind you and fall back on your tush," our guide told us after strapping us into life jackets. "Stay to your right. When you see the campground, that's the take-out point. If you're too far out into the river, you won't get over in time, and who knows where you'll be able to get out. The river's moving pretty fast. About four miles per hour."

Four mph. Huh. A snail's pace compared to the Turner.

The girls stopped their nervous-Nellie chattering long enough to flop back on their fannies. We were off.

Slowly.

But speed was not the name of this game. Relaxing was. Within five minutes we began to ease back and allow ourselves to go with the flow. When the I-84 overpass disappeared from sight, the tubes began to passively revolve with the current, and we were lost in a primeval setting in which the riverbanks were thick with trees and undergrowth, the crickets made the dominant noise, and worldly cares slipped away.

Until the gurgling rumble assaulted our ears.

"What's that?" cried Nancy. She'd drifted ahead of us and now suddenly remembered that she was supposed to be terrified.

"Rapids," I said.

"Laina!" Nancy screeched. "Laina, let me hold your hand."

I shouldn't have called them rapids. Ripples? Whatever you'd call baby rapids. Bobbing through them, we were lightly shaken, then placed back on the river's table-smooth surface. Cute – once Nancy had stopped screeching.

Try a raft, tube, or canoe to travel down the Delaware

We drifted on. I lolled into a reverie. An island appeared. Stay to the right. I saw visions of pioneers canoeing the river long before campgrounds and highways and summer resorts were invented. I saw the entangled underbrush and trees. I saw myself drifting to the river's center. I saw the water's eddies whorl and move on. I saw a hawk circling. I saw the girls floating in to the take-out point.

Whoa! Take-out point? What am I doing here at midstream?

Whoa! I flapped my arms and kicked my feet like a mad duck. No progress. Suddenly, 4 mph wasn't so lazy. The girls were out of the water. But, yikes, I was going to miss it!

Splush. I tipped myself over and, clutching the tube like a swimming pool kickboard, I kicked and flapped a free arm. I gauged the distance (twenty yards?) against the current's strength, then kicked harder. And kicked bottom. The water was barely waist high. I stood and caught my breath. Panic? Who, me? Coolly, I strolled to shore.

"I thought you weren't going to make it!" Laina yelped.

"Piece of cake," I lied. Did I say tubing wasn't going to be exciting?

Specifically: The Delaware Water Gap National Recreation Area runs for thirty-seven miles in both New Jersey and Pennsylvania. The southern visitors' center is located on the New Jersey side at Kittatinny Point (908-496-4458) just off I-80. The northern Dingmans Falls Visitor Center (717-828-7802) is on the Pennsylvania side at Dingmans Ferry. Both centers offer extensive programming; call for information and a schedule of events.

The Gap provides facilities for launching boats, fishing, camping, swimming, picnicking, hunting, and, in winter, snowshoeing and cross-country skiing. Bicyclists will enjoy riding along Old Mine Road. Some twenty operations rent canoes.

Among the tubing companies: Indian Head Canoes and Rafts in Newton, NJ, 1-800-874-2628; Delaware River Camping Resort in Delaware, NJ, 201-475-4517 or 1-800-543-0271; Kittatinny Canoes, Dingmans Ferry, PA, 1-800-356-2852.

Lodging is available at the Old Mine Road Youth Hostel (201-948-6750).

12 Horsing Around
Hackettstown

This is about the size of it—I've never trusted any animal that's significantly larger than I am. Take horses, for example. You never know when one might decide to remind you who's boss. No matter how much you can bench press in your basement, you'll lose.

Little girls, on the other hand, never seem to have this problem. I don't get it. Within an hour of arriving at a stables or guest ranch, my daughter is addressing every one of the dozens of horses in the corral by name, petting and cooing at them. I'm still calling them "Sir" and "Ma'am" when we leave—whether that's three hours or three days later. And how come the daughter—who has only been on a horse a half dozen times in her life—is off and cantering before I can figure out how to get my twenty-eight-short leg high enough in the air to put my foot in the stirrup? And how come my wife is laughing?

We've ridden, if we can call it that, in exotic locales such as Colorado and the state of Washington, but you don't have to go way out west to play cowboy. One early spring day, we stumbled into a most unlikely looking place just outside Hackettstown, right next to US 46. "Horizon Stables," the handmade-looking sign read. "Horseback Riding." The place didn't look like much—a barn that seemed to have seen better days was all we could see from the highway. Still, it was such a surprise to see a stable sitting so near to the highway we had to investigate.

We turned right, drove a few hundred feet, and pulled over. A variety of vehicles and horse trailers were parked in a disorderly fashion. I stepped out of the car, and stepped right into . . . it. I'd forgotten. Near horses, you've got to watch your step, and there were plenty of horses around. Most of them stood nonchalantly swiping their tails at invisible flies. Plenty of riders were hanging around, too, mostly young and female.

Some sat on a fence that surrounded a riding ring. Others fussed over the animals. Beyond the barn, a large open field drifted up a lazy hill. Thick woods loomed in the distance.

Horizon, it turns out, is one of the few places in northern New Jersey that runs full-fledged trail rides. "Hack riding," Megan LaBrie called it. A twenty-one-year-old equestrienne and native of Hackettstown, Megan was working as a stablehand at Horizon while she trained for the pro rodeo circuit. "We're also one of the few stables that emphasizes Western riding," she pointed out. Rides cover most of the property, some fifty acres, and offer access to about ten miles of wooded and pastured trails. A popular ride follows a circuit around a nearby reservoir. "Plus," Megan added cheerfully, "we can go out on the power-line cuts—you know, where the electric company has run those high voltage power lines? There's miles of 'em around here."

I wasn't so sure I'd want to ride under the invisible electrical fields of the power lines, but Megan was undaunted. She liked going out on rides "that are special, or, you know, different." Indeed, she described several rides in which the horses were "trailered" to the starting points. "We do trailer rides to the gorge in Califon, and we ride along the old railroad bed that runs from High Bridge to Mount Olive," Megan related enthusiastically. "Last year, we trailered to another stable and then did a ride up to Waterloo Village during their Oktoberfest. After we spent the day there, we rode back. It was five and a half hours of riding."

For those who are too young or too timid, pony rides are offered.

Horseback riding is popular throughout the state, from suburban settings such as Bergen County's Overpeck County Park or the Saddle Ridge Riding Center in Franklin Lakes, to places at the beach like Hidden Valley Ranch in Cape May, or in the mountains, of which there are many.

We refrained from riding that day—we had other commitments—but we watched a group go out over the pasture. Like our own kid, they looked like they'd been born atop those enormous steeds. Actually, even if you're a horse sissy like me, there's nothing to worry about. Most of these rent-a-horse run on automatic. They have to. After all, they've got to handle a lot of petrified novices like me. And you know what they say about horses. They can feel your fear through the seat of your pants. Which is why I always call them "Sir."

Specifically: Horizon Stables (908-852-9509) is open year-round on US 46 in Hackettstown.

The New Jersey Division of Travel and Tourism's Outdoor Guide lists many riding stables and the state parks that allow riding; call 1-800-537-7397 for a copy.

13 Birdwatching
Dennisville

Marty Thurlow loves to tell bird-watcher stories. He'll sit with you in the sun room of the Henry Ludlam Inn, a bed and breakfast he runs with his wife, Ann, in one of Cape May County's oldest houses, and gladly regale you with tales of the ardor, fervor, and obsession displayed by people dedicated to sighting our winged friends. To a person unschooled in the ways of birdwatching, these narratives make fascinating listening, especially when enjoyed over a cup of Ann Thurlow's hot apple cider.

In the spring, people flock to the Dennisville area. They do it because the birds flock here, too, and the birds do it because the horseshoe crabs flock here. Some mind-boggling statistics: horseshoe crabs, large-shelled animals that look like miniature Panzer tanks, predate the dinosaurs by about 150 million years and are considered by some to be living fossils. These crabs live only in the Atlantic Ocean, and they nest primarily on the lower Delaware Bay. More than a million shorebirds depend upon the eggs laid by the crabs for springtime survival. The birds consume approximately 300 tons of the nutritious eggs each spring.

Take the Red Knot, for example. It flies nonstop for four days from the southern reaches of Argentina to reach the Delaware Bay feast, makes a two-week rest stop here, during which it doubles its weight, and then flies on another 3,000 miles to nest in the Canadian arctic.

A significant portion of this crab/bird activity takes place just down the road from the Henry Ludlam Inn at an inauspicious spot called Reed's Beach, which is why it's hard to get a room at the inn come spring.

The road to Reed's Beach is accessible from State 47 and runs for 2.5 miles through marshes thick with the area's signature wildgrasses and reeds. It then takes you past an eerie place where the road is lined on one side with the skeletons of dead trees and on the other with high, almost desert-like sand dunes. You know you've reached the famous birding spot when the road ends. (Bring bug spray. Reed's Beach has also gained fame for its thick mosquito and biting bug population.)

In truth, there's great birding all along the Delaware Bay in this region that I've come to call the "underbelly of New Jersey." To me, it is the most remarkable area of a remarkably diverse state. But like so much of New Jersey, the region too often serves only as a byway to other places. With the exception of a small handful of fishermen, duck hunters, and boaters (and birders), most people are just passing through. The birders will tell you, however, there's a lot of reasons to stop and, well, smell the wetlands.

Dennisville's long and active history begins with cedar mining. Long ago, enormous cedar trees grew in the nearby swamps, gaining heights as tall as the famous western redwoods. But at some point, a violent storm (or storms) felled nearly all the grand old trees, and they eventually sank into the swamp. Being submerged and overgrown with peat, the cedar wood remained remarkably preserved. When Europeans migrated into the area, they discovered the trunks and dug them up. Thus, the term cedar mining, instead of cedar lumbering. From these trees were made many a seagoing ship, as well as the shingles that top the roof of Independence Hall in Philadelphia, but inevitably, one day the cedar was played out.

Sand mines were another enterprise that supported the area's economy. A number of them can still be found nearby along County 660. The sand was taken up the road to Millville – site of Wheaton Village and the Glass Museum (see Chapter 48) – where it was made into glass.

When you travel to the area today, you enter a world that feels far closer to the rural south than it does to the familiar industrialized environment we associate with New Jersey. Follow

County 553 through the lush overgrowth of semitropical plants to tiny Port Norris, and you'll feel as though you've traveled to the areas outside North Carolina's Hilton Head. Head south from there to the minuscule hamlet of Bivalve, and you'll find the remnants of the oystering business that once thrived in the bay. It's making a comeback of sorts, but the locals will tell you it's nothing like it used to be.

Continue east on County 553 to the tiny town of Dividing Creek, stop in at the marina that sits next to the highway along the banks of Dividing Creek, and ask for a boat tour. Perhaps you can rent a boat and travel up the Maurice (pronounced Morris) River, through the dense vegetation and unique ecology that has led to the river's being designated as a National Wild and Scenic River. Or perhaps you'd rather just keep driving along Methodist Road and down County 643 to the microscopic bayside community of Gandy's Beach. These small, rural hamlets, proverbial one-horse towns that seem to be from a different time and light-years away from the helter-skelter, traffic-laden world of suburban shopping malls, are a study in themselves, and they all provide access to excellent birding.

Meanwhile, back at Reed's Beach, you'll find a handwritten sign (assuming it has survived the last winter) that offers bird-watching boat tours. Me, I'd get into one of those boats and watch the bird watchers. As Marty Thurlow says, they put on quite a show in their own right.

Specifically: The Henry Ludlam Inn (609-861-5847) is located on State 47 in Dennisville. Take the Garden State Parkway Exit 13, turn north on US 9, then go west on State 83 and west on State 47. From the inn you'll have easy access to Reed's Beach, all the Bay towns, Cape May, and many other shore points, plus you can canoe the private lake or bird watch from the gazebo and swing in the backyard.

14 The Native American Arts Festival
Powhatan Renape Nation Reservation, Rancocas

The five men, dressed in colorful, ceremonial costumes, solemnly encircle the pole and momentarily honor it with ritualistic gravity. Then, methodically, they begin to climb into the sky. At the pole's zenith—100 feet off the ground—they adeptly take their places. Four of them seat themselves on a square frame rigged to the pole. The fifth stands on the narrow surface of the very top. Now, the top man begins to play a handmade wooden flute and an attached miniature drum. The flute's trilled resonance and the drum's persistent beat float down over the gathered crowd who stare up fascinated, from below. The flute player dances, rotating in that precarious spot on sure, rapidly moving feet. Suddenly, as one, the four others fall backward, like deep-sea divers dropping into midair. Their fall is abrupt, but short. Just as suddenly, they are dangling from ropes. Slowly, hanging upside down, they rotate gently clockwise around the pole. The flute and drum music continues. Like spiders letting out silk, the ropes grow gradually longer, lowering the four men toward the ground while the flute and drum play on. When they are within head-height of the grass, the men flip over as one and touch ground.

The pole dance of Mexico's Totaneko Indians is the most daring event at the Powhatan Renape Nation's Native American Arts Festival, but it may not be the most spectacular, depending upon your personal point of view.

You might think, rather, that the fire dance creates a greater spectacle. Performers dressed in flashy, bright combinations of black and white, wearing colorful feather headdresses that wave gracefully with their movements, dance dangerously close to fiery flame pots accompanied by hard-driving drums.

Or, perhaps, you find the intricate movement of the hoop

dancer, as she weaves several colorful wooden rings into a variety of geometric patterns, more of a spectacle. No matter. The Arts Festival's nonstop entertainment leaves you little time to ponder what is most daring or spectacular.

The Powhatan Renape Nation's Rankokus Reservation occupies 350 wooded acres along the Rancocas River, just a few minutes from a commercial highway strip that seems worlds away. The Powhatan are one of the oldest documented tribes in North America. They lived in the midAtlantic regions of Maryland and Delaware when the Europeans arrived. They hold two of the oldest treaties signed by Native Americans with Europeans, including one signed with England in 1646. Although the Powhatan Renape's forty nations signed a 1677 treaty that gave them rights to vast amounts of Virginia, they, like most Native American nations, were slowly driven off their lands. In time, many Powhatan settled in the Delaware Valley. In the mid-1980s, with the designation of this tract in southern New Jersey as the official Rankokus Reservation, these Delaware Valley Powhatan finally had a place to call their own.

Each year during Memorial Day weekend (and again on Columbus Day weekend), the reservation hosts the largest juried Native American arts festival east of Santa Fe, New Mexico. With sixty booths, a large performing stage, and many exhibition areas and animal displays, the reservation's great central field comes alive with everything from art and buffalo burgers to alligator wrestling and traditional storytelling.

The Powhatan's Festival celebrates the Native American way of life. The art, crafts, blankets, and other works that are judged and sold here are created in the old ways by working artist masters who sell what they make for a living. The dances, rites, and ceremonies date back to ancient times, and reflect the vitality, excitement, and depth of the Indian traditions. Tepees and traditional thatch huts bring the old ways to life and illustrate how the tribes lived in harmony with nature. Wisdom Keepers share tribal histories and folklore, and answer questions about the Native American perceptions of life and way of being. Potters, bow-makers, and mask-makers demonstrate their skills and techniques. Cooks prepare delicious customary foods such as fried bread, alligator burgers, buffalo burgers, and much more that keep visitors coming back for more.

At each festival, an eagle or an owl, having been nursed back to health after injury, is released into the wild. As the majestic bird flies back to freedom, a rush of elation touches all who see it go. The bird symbolizes man's connection to nature. It also serves as a metaphor: that the injured people's nation, like the injured soaring raptor, can be returned to full health and live life to the fullest once again.

The Arts Festival highlights the year's activities on the Rankokus Reservation, but the reservation is open year-round. It houses a small museum that contains seventeen beautiful dioramas. Hand-rendered and modeled by the museum's founder, Charles Danse, the scenes illustrate the Powhatan Renape Nation's history, lifestyle, and survival techniques. The museum also contains an art gallery that holds some exceptional pieces. Outdoors, a short nature trail explores the shores of the Rancocas River. A printed guide not only identifies plant species, but helps you understand how the wilderness's plants and animals function within the Indian philosophy of life: that all Earth Creatures live in harmony. A harmony that's easy to imagine in a setting like this.

Specifically: The Powhatan Renape Nation's Rankokus Reservation (609-261-4747) is located on Rancocas Road in Rancocas. From the New Jersey Turnpike Exit 5, make a right turn onto County 541, drive about two miles and turn right onto County 541-Spur. Go to the next traffic light and turn right onto Rancocas Road; the reservation is just less than two miles on the left. From I-295, take Exit 45A and follow Rancocas Road toward Mt. Holly. The reservation is on the right in about three-quarters of a mile. Call for museum hours and an Arts Festival schedule.

15 Island Beach State Park

Of all the 100-plus miles of New Jersey shore, Island Beach State Park is my favorite spot. It's quiet, pristine, pleasant, and unpretentious. No place in New Jersey offers you the chance to experience the ocean, the dunes, the wildlife, the native flora – indeed the whole natural package – more completely than this.

Island Beach's tradition as a preserve dates back to the 1930s, when a man named Francis Freeman gained control over the old Henry Phipps estate. Phipps had conceived of the land as a seaside paradise for the prosperous, but Freeman gave precedence to nature's abundance rather than human affluence. While Phipps had constructed three large houses for his intended guests, Freeman restricted visitors to those who would act with constraint. No berry picking, destroying the dunes, or otherwise despoiling the area's natural resources. Day fishermen, hunters, and strollers were welcome.

During the '40s, the War Department took control of the area and kicked everyone out so they could experiment with antiaircraft rocketry. In 1953, the land became a state park and preserve. Today, the area's condition is not very much different from what the first European explorers might have found.

In my younger years, I was a moody young man, and there were more than a few occasions when I came to Island Beach to seek solace from my worldly woes by indulging in long beach walks and hours of pondering life's imponderables beside the surf's ebb and flow. When I return these days, as a husband, father, and hardworking adult, more given to wrestling with life's day-to-day hassles than its ambiguities, I still find refreshing solace here.

The park offers only 2,400 parking spaces, so while the lifeguarded beach areas can become crowded, you need not walk far to get away from the crowds. (Not to swim, however. Swimming along unguarded beaches is always a bad idea.) The patrolled beaches offer full bathhouses with changing facilities and snack bars. These are clean and simple, in keeping with the overall atmosphere of the park. Even in the swimming areas, tubes and other inflatables are forbidden. Surfing is restricted to the more southerly patrolled areas, which helps to maintain a low-key atmosphere.

Just a short walk from the swimming beaches, the beach-combing and strolling become incomparable. Depending upon the time of year, you'll likely come up with some fascinating shells, sea horses, starfish, or other treasures.

As you wander south, you'll find that legal beach access via four-wheel-drive vehicles makes this prime surf fishing territory. Casting for bluefish is especially good in the fall, which you might want to keep in mind if your ability to handle the sway of the deep-water party boats is, like mine, limited (see Chapter 7). You can count on finding lots of people there to regale you with fish stories for as long as you can listen to them.

The entire park is just under ten miles long, with a single two-lane road running down its middle, almost to the southern end.

The welcome center lies only a mile from the entrance. Also known as the Aeolium, it offers a wealth of maps and other park information. Just beyond its doors, you can explore the dunes with a short self-guided hike on the nature trail; park naturalists lead guided hikes during the summer. The eel grasses are especially interesting; they were once harvested to make insulation for houses and upholstery stuffing for Model-T Fords. The park's terrain is almost completely flat, providing casual and relaxing bike riding. Indeed, bike riders can enter the park for free.

When you get to the southern end of the park, you're across the inlet from Barnegat Lighthouse, an exceptionally pretty spot. If you're certified to scuba dive and can verify it, the southern oceanfront beach areas offer prime diving.

But more than anything, Island Beach presents a chance to walk in wonderment. It offers an opportunity to view the Jersey shore in its native condition, back in the times when white sand beaches, coastal scrub forest, and barrier sand dunes encouraged wildlife-preserving sanctuary and habitat, not commercial development. The beach provides a place to contemplate the larger powers that work the planet.

If, after all this naturalness, the urge to get funky and revel in honky-tonk just cannot be subjugated, the bustling Seaside boardwalk is just a few minutes away by car.

Specifically: Island Beach State Park (908-793-0506) is open year-round from 8:00 A.M. to 8:00 P.M. The beach bathhouses are open from Memorial Day to Labor Day. To reach the park, take the Garden State Parkway to Exit 82; follow State 37 east across Barnegat Bay, then go south on State 35 through Seaside Heights and Seaside Park. Call ahead for information on fishing license and diving permits.

16 The Cowtown Rodeo
Woodstown

Professional rodeo? In New Jersey? You betcha! Every Saturday night, the Cowtown Rodeo rides into Woodstown, no more than eight miles from the Delaware Memorial Bridge.

Pro rodeo in New Jersey may surprise most folks, but the locals come out in droves to watch the cowboys and cowgirls rope, wrestle, and ride. Traffic on US 40 backs up for a mile in either direction of the entrance. The glow of the rodeo ring arc lights can be seen from several miles away. Little kids sit with their noses pressed to the wire fence that surrounds the riding ring. Teenagers, dressed to the country and western nines in their jeans, checkered shirts, high-heeled cowboy boots, and, yes, their Stetsons, exchange all the appealing and furtive glances and feigned nonchalance that pervade high school dances. Folks of all ages arrive in their RVs (recreational vehicles) to whoop and holler and make like this was Wyoming.

Arriving just at showtime, we winced when we saw the line at the little white and red wooden ticket booth. It stretched back a good twenty yards. We followed a procession of other late-arriving cars and were directed by a plump young woman in a police-like uniform to a parking spot in a grassy field.

"Do they stop selling tickets at a certain number?" we asked her, unsure if we'd get in after making the long drive south.

"Nah," she replied with a smile. "They'll just keep sellin' 'em till there's nobody left to buy 'em."

"Can we bring our cooler in?"

"Well, little coolers are okay. Just ask at the gate. They'll let you know if it's too big."

The Cowtown Rodeo, it turns out, is a BYOB affair. While you can buy hot dogs, popcorn, candy apples, soda, hot funnel cake, ice cream, and other vital vittles at the concession stands, the rodeo sells no beer. You're welcome to bring your own, however, which everyone seems to do. If your cooler's too big, you just leave it by the fence and come back to it when you need to.

We parked our cooler, paid our admission, and wandered up the grassy knoll to join the crowd. The onlookers loomed above us, standing three deep behind those who were seated. Broad-brimmed cowboy hats were silhouetted against the flood-lights. We slithered into a spot where we could see the ring. It seemed small. A bright white wooden "grandstand," with blazing crimson trim, offered prime "box seat" views high along one side. It held just four or five rows of seats within its enclosure. Ringside, people sat on rows of wooden benches that had been set into the side of a shallow hill. At one end, an announcer's booth overlooked all; at the other, cattle of various sorts stood in pens below ring level patiently waiting to be ushered into the spotlight.

Despite being outdoors, smoke hung heavy in the air. Also, pervading everything, was the pungent redolence that can only mean horses and cattle. Some folks go for that acidic combina-tion of hide, hair, and manure. Not me.

The rodeo started with a grand entry parade. After that, eight events made up the night's card – just about everything you'd expect in a rodeo from bareback riding to steer wrestling. For the riding events, the program – a typed legal-sized sheet of paper – graciously listed the animals' names as well as the riders'. Who would dare ride a bull named Jalapeno!

Our favorite event was the girls' barrel race. Four barrels were set up, and the women had to ride from one end of the arena to the other and back again, going around each barrel along the way. The young women were excellent riders, but we particularly liked the fact that the event was a straightforward

*A barrel racer pits her riding ability and the speed of
her horse against the clock*

display of skill that involving no victimized animals—no busting, roping, or wrestling some poor animal who'd probably rather be out munching on grass anyway.

Despite continued cajoling by the announcer and antics of the old reliable rodeo clowns, the crowd didn't appear to be paying a lot of attention. Eating, chatting, and shopping seemed to get a lot of play. Western wear, western hats, cowboy toys and trinkets, and T-shirts were being sold, and the souvenir stands seemed to be doing a brisk business.

Despite the crowd's low-key attitude, this was true professional rodeo, complete with prize money and skilled athletes, and the crowd did cheer loudly when a cowboy performed well. Many of these cowboys have had some success on the major-league rodeo circuit, and their skills were impressive. The only one who gave me pause was the one bucking bronco rider who was announced as hailing from the Bronx. An urban cowboy, I suppose.

Specifically: The Cowtown Rodeo (609-769-3200) can be found on US 40 in Woodstown; it can be reached from Exit 1 or 2 off the New Jersey Turnpike. From Exit 1, follow US 40 east for eight miles. From Exit 2, take US 322 east to Mullica Hill, then follow State 45 south into Woodstown; turn right when you get into the center of town and right again onto US 40 west.

The rodeo rides every Saturday evening at 7:30 P.M. from Memorial Day through September. Tickets are sold on a first-come first-served basis. On Sundays, the rodeo grounds host one of South Jersey's biggest flea markets.

17 Fore! Golf House Museum, Far Hills; And the State's Best Courses

I set my feet, tightened my grip, and lined up the club head with the ball. I waggled the club, my feet, and my tush, just like the pros do on TV. I checked the fairway one more time, then oh-so-slowly brought the club up and back. Now! I swiped a grand arc forward and down, shooting my good intentions along the club shaft through the head and down to the ball, creating a grand sweeping flow that oozed with power and perfect form. I anticipated the Whack! but all I got was a dull thud. The dirt-scuffed ball dribbled over the blanched ground like a wounded woodchuck, leaving behind a torrent of flying turf and a divot bigger than my swelled hopes.

Why does anyone play this game?

You might not find the answer to that question at Golf House in Far Hills, but you will find some answers to questions like these: How is a golf ball made? How was a golf ball made in 1620? How far will a modern golf ball travel on the moon if hit at a specified force? What is acceptable and unacceptable in the design of golf clubs?

Golf House is the headquarters of the United States Golf Association (USGA). Anyone who generally enjoys golf, or who can appreciate the game as a measure of social history, should visit this extremely pleasant, pastoral site.

Set in a mansion of Georgian colonial design, amid fittingly fairway-like lawns, Golf House takes you on a magic carpet ride through the sport's history. The game's roots reach as far back as Rome, but it began to flower at the turn of the sixteenth century. Golf's first public written record, we learn, was in the Acts of the Scots Parliament, circa 1497. Did the Scotsmen issue an official state edict outlining proper play? No. They prohibited the game. The decree didn't take. All of the Stuart kings and queens (1502–1688), including Mary, Queen of Scots, were hackers.

Golf House presents much more of this fascinating quasi-social history, reviewing the development of clubs (how a "brassie" became a 2-iron), balls, and golfwear, as well as how the sand tee was replaced by the wooden one.

The USGA is the game's American governing body. Among other things, it sets the rules and standards for equipment and guidelines for course development, and its Research and Test Center is located adjacent to the museum. There, you'll learn how exactingly balls are made and, equally as meticulously, tested, as well as what's legal and illegal in club design. If the weather's good, you might see Iron Byron working out on the practice tee. Byron's a robot, you see, whose only job is to smack golf balls with such an invariable swing (speed, force, and loft) that their performance characteristics can be evaluated against a measurable standard.

You really needn't be a golfer to appreciate Golf House, but if you are a golfer, watch out. By the time you leave the grounds, you'll be itching to play, and there are some very playable public courses in New Jersey. Among them:

NORTH

Crystal Springs Golf Club
Hamburg
This is a hilly, challenging course set in an old quarry that lends a very unique character. Crystal Springs has been described as extremely challenging, or as one person put it, "It's a 'must play,' but bring lots of balls." Information: 201-827-1444.

Great Gorge Country Club/Season's Resort
McAfee
Season's Resort started life years ago as the Playboy Club and,

after a number of unsuccessful rebirths, it has hit prosperity under its current management. An amenity-laden, full-service resort hotel, Season's offers its guests reduced-rate golf at the nearby Great Gorge Country Club. The club offers twenty-seven picturesque holes that combine wooded, lakeside, and quarry-side settings and a variety of challenge that will capture any golfer's fancy. Information: Season's, 201-827-6000 or 1-800-835-2555; Great Gorge Country Club, 201-827-5757.

CENTRAL SHORE

Marriott's Seaview Resort
Galloway Township
Seaview provides a classic club setting. It was once an exclusive private club where the likes of Dwight Eisenhower liked to play a round. With two championship courses, a gleaming white neoclassic building (described in the brochures as "Gatsby-esque"), all the services a first-class hotel or country club should offer, and a location fifteen minutes' drive from Atlantic City— Seaview has it all. *Golf Digest* ranks Seaview's Pines Course among New Jersey's best. On the Bay Course, the tight oceanside links with its bunker-fortified greens might have you thinking you're playing the classic Scottish game. Information: 1-800-932-8000 or 609-748-1990.

Blue Heron Pines Golf Club
Galloway Township
Blue Heron Pines aspires to a private club ambience. By all reports, it has succeeded. With an excellent restaurant, clean and comfortable locker rooms, and an understated modern architectural design, the club makes you feel welcome. The course isn't too shabby either, designed by accomplished archi-

tect Stephen Kay. The Atlantic City area abounds with excellent courses, and Blue Heron is among the best of them. Information: 609-965-1800.

CENTRAL

Howell Park Golf Course
Farmingdale
Despite a tendency to be crowded on weekends, Howell Park engenders rave reviews from golfers of all types. So impressive are the links that *Golf Digest* has ranked the course among the top fifty public courses in America. This very challenging course is well kept and a pleasure to play. Information: 908-938-4771.

Hominy Hill Golf Club
Colts Neck
Hominy Hill does Howell one better, having been ranked in *Golf Digest's* top twenty-five public courses in America. A Robert Trent Jones design, the course is considered long and difficult, but it's very playable even when it gets crowded. Many New Jersey golfers will tell you this is the best public course in the state. Information: 908-462-9222.

SOUTH

Cape May National Golf Club
Cape May
What would you expect from a course that lies near the queen city of the southern New Jersey shore? Wind, water, and plenty of sand. That's Cape May National. Cape May is a delightful

course that includes a memorable par 3 set beside a nature preserve. Information: 609-884-1563.

Specifically: Golf House (908-234-2300) is located on Liberty Corner Road in Far Hills. Hours are 10:00 A.M. to 4:00 P.M. on weekends, and 9:00 A.M. to 5:00 P.M. weekdays. To reach Golf House, take I-287 to Exit 18, then follow US 206 north to US 202 north, then to County 512 east, and then follow the signs. From I-78, take Exit 33, follow County 525 north to County 512 west.

The New Jersey Division of Travel and Tourism's Outdoor Guide lists the state's public access golf courses. Call 1-800-537-7397 to obtain a copy.

18 The Sussex County Farm and Horse Show
Sussex

You see a lot of animals at the Sussex County Farm and Horse Show, but me, I could've watched the racing miniature pigs forever. First of all, they're sooo cute! Secondly, they're ridiculous. Tiny porkers all done up in little racing bibs, they run around the small oval while their masters recite a running commentary. Lastly, I'm a sucker for miniaturized anything, even pigs.

The Sussex County Farm and Horse Show takes place for ten days in early August. It may represent a last gasp attempt to maintain contact with New Jersey's agrarian roots. Long may it live.

Only once, when I was perhaps seven or eight, did I have the opportunity to attend one of the classic midwestern state fairs. You know, those large and exuberant gatherings where country music stars sing, where farmers put their equipment and animals to a public test by using them to pull enormous amounts of weight, where blueberry pies (and anything else that can be baked, cooked, or grown) are judged, and where the smarmy farm smells pervade even the food and game midways, and nobody seems to mind. Well, the Sussex County Farm and Horse Show is as close as we New Jerseyans come to something like that.

When my older kid, Dan, was just six or so, he went absolutely bonkers over the mud races. That perfectly ordinary folks were trying to drive cars and trucks with gargantuan wheels through a man-made bog seemed totally sensible to him. To me, it was clear that this was just the grown-ups' extension of playing with trucks in the sandbox, but the boy loved it. And so did dozens of other little (and not so little) boys and girls, too.

You say you'd rather watch oxen pull stuff than tractors? You can do that, too. And whether you like your pulling done by animals or machines, you'll love your destruction carried out by men in machines. Don't miss the Demolition Derby.

Our girl child, Laina, preferred the horse ring. The fair puts on a horse show of some kind each day—a Quarter Horse Show, a Welsh & Crossbred Pony Show, a Team Pulling Contest, an Arabian and Half-Arabian Show, and so on.

As to Mom, well, I don't think she had a particular favorite. I think the whole affair reminded her of being a kid back at the county fair in rural California. I guess that's the whole point of the Sussex Show, the reason it stands out. There's nothing pretentious here. It's refreshing to know that there are still kids out there who raise blue-ribbon rabbits and roosters; that farmers still exist in New Jersey who will transport a heifer for miles in an effort to win Best in Show; that women will cook carefully guarded family recipes just to chase a blue ribbon. Sure, the show has a lot of tacky stuff—the usual array of booths filled with buy-it-anywhere trinkets and pseudo-crafts and the requisite junk food vendors who first soak their wares in grease then soak you if you want to buy them. But a carney element is not only to be expected, it's welcomed.

Everyone who has any kind of talent is likely to show up to show off. The Performing Arts Tent echoes with the sounds of music and, well, dogs—the "Tails-A-Waggin' Dog Act," "Canine Companions" and the "Corky & Riker Dog Act" are just a few of the typical doggone events. Human entertainers range from the Crossroads Assembly of God Adult Choir and Worship Team to the Blue Ribbon Cloggers & Pony Express Dancers and the Jersey Junior Karate Academy.

Antique farm machinery, a petting zoo, a milking parlor, and the exhibition building (where photography, home economics, flower, horticultural, and honey shows are featured) are also on-going features at Sussex.

Now, some debate has been riffling up at our house. Seems

the young 'uns want to challenge my notion that miniature pig racing is the top event of the show. They're purporting that the combination event of the Pot Belly Pig Confirmation Show and the Pen Decorating Contest takes the blue ribbon for best attraction. And suddenly Mom, knowing my affection for miniatures, reminds me that the miniature horse show deserves recognition. But, I say, you haven't seen anything until you've seen those tiny porklets going around the far turn dashing for glory and victory. Just take in a few of these races and then wander over to the Livestock Area for the Open Swine Show, and you'll know just what it means to be as happy as a pig . . . .

Specifically: The Sussex County Farm and Horse Show (201-948-0540) takes place during early August at the fairgrounds on Plains Road in Augusta. To get there, take I-80 to Exit 34B, then follow State 15 north to US 206 north, and continue one mile to Plains Road. Or take State 23 north into Sussex and turn left onto County 639 south to County 565 south; follow the signs onto Linn Road to Plains Road.

19 Long Beach Island

Some eighteen miles long but barely three blocks wide at its narrow points, Long Beach Island ranks among the most popular summer beach vacation spots for northern New Jerseyans. You've got to wonder why an island of this size is divided into twenty-one individual communities. Some, like Beach Haven Crest and North Beach Haven, stretch for less than ten blocks. But nobody seems to regard these lines as anything more than designations on a map. The island offers isolation as well as access, quietude and activity, and a blend of full-time residents, summer-home owners, and overnight lodges.

We left our rooms at the Engleside Inn, a large and comfortable motel in Beach Haven at the island's southern reaches, and began a bicycle exploration. The riding is straight and flat. Bike lanes along Atlantic and Beach Avenues (each one-way streets) make this section's north-south riding easy and safe even in the busiest times. In case you've come unprepared but get a sudden urge to ride, a number of island shops rent bikes.

Another kind of riding vehicle can be rented, as well— jetskis or waverunners, those snowmobiles for the water. Jetskiing isn't calm or contemplative; it's high action. While some regard the fast-flying little vehicles to be as pesky as flies at a picnic, even their staunchest critics must admit driving them is a lot of fun. Looking for less mechanized action? Windsurfing gear can be rented at Ocean Kayak in Brant Beach. If jetskiing is water snowmobiling, then windsurfing is on-water downhill skiing.

Our ride, however, was meant to be leisurely. We rolled to where the *Black Whales* is docked and checked the schedules. The boat departs twice a day for a nine-hour excursion and play-day (or night) in Atlantic City. Alas, you must be twenty-one to ride, but you needn't be a grown-up to take the evening bay cruise. The *Black Whales* offers three one-hour sightseeing rides on the island's bay side, plus daily fishing excursions, on summer weekdays only.

We turned back toward the mid-island. At the corner of Beach Avenue and Engleside Street, the sidewalk turns to neatly laid red brick. The brick walk leads to the Surflight Theater. Through the summer and into October, the theater offers high-caliber live shows, usually tuneful musicals. Right next door stands Show Place, an ice cream parlor of local renown where singing waitpeople serve your order with an operatic flair.

We drifted across the street to the Long Beach Island Historical Museum, a weathered wooden building that holds a wealth of area cultural history. The photos of the 1962 nor'easter, in particular, tell a fascinating tale of nature's devastating power.

Speaking of history, over at 9th and Bay Avenue, the Schooner's Wharf shopping center takes its theme from the two-masted schooner *Lucy Evelyn*. Permanently moored at this spot in 1948 and transformed into a gift shop, the ship is now the focal point of the shopping plaza which, with its planking and weathered woods, has adapted the nautical design. Along with Bay Village across the street, the complex provides the island's shopping hub. It also hosts spectacular fireworks for July 4th and a handful of October events like the "Chowderfest" and the "Festa di Columbo 18-Mile Run," a combination of Italian cuisine carbo-loading pigout followed by a high-energy calorie-burning atonement.

Next door are Fantasy Island and Thundering Surf Water Park. Fantasy Island is a family-friendly amusement park. Clean and small, the rides delight young children and keep their parents from dying of fear for their safety. You pay by the ride here, so it can be as expensive or affordable as the limits you set. A "family casino arcade" offers an electronic mini-Atlantic City. As to Thundering Surf, according to an "undisclosed" youthful source I know (who has the experience to speak authoritatively), the water park can be classified as "totally cool."

Still, it is the beach that makes LBI special. It's pure, no frills, and importantly, barrier-free and accessible for people with disabilities. The island contains thirty access ramps and the various communities combine to provide twenty "beach wheels"– wheelchairs suitable for use on the beach and in the surf– making this one of the most accessible beaches on the shore.

The island's northern end is essentially residential and sedate. From Bayview Avenue on the bay side of Barnegat Light, you can board one of several deep-sea-fishing vessels (see Chapter 7), or just buy yourself some fish. A drive along 12th Street reveals a series of houses built in the 1880s, and a stop at the corner of 5th Street and Central Avenue is always worthwhile. That's the Barnegat Light Museum, formerly a one-room schoolhouse.

Continue up to the northern end of the island, and you come to the real Barnegat Light–the lighthouse. Barnegat Lighthouse State Park covers thirty-one acres on the island's tip. Its newly renovated and barrier-free facilities offer picnicking, fishing, and pleasant seaside strolling. Of course, you can climb the lighthouse steps. The lighthouse, known to the locals as "Old Barney," stands 172 feet high; it overlooks Barnegat Shoals, the site of some 200 shipwrecks over the years. Indeed, the name "Barnegat" derives from the Dutch name for the inlet–"Barendegat"–which meant "inlet of breakers," a homage to the treacherous nature of the narrow water passageway that connects Barnegat Bay to the ocean.

LBI is a quiet island with spectacular scenery, historical sites, and a user-friendly beach that's walking distance from almost anyplace, unfettered by commercial glut, and yet not far from commercial facilities. No wonder my neighbors flock here.

Specifically: For general, regional information on Long Beach Island, contact the Southern Ocean County Chamber of Commerce, 265 West 9th Street, Ship Bottom, NJ 08008; phone 1-800-292-6372 or 609-494-7211.

To get there, take the Garden State Parkway to Exit 63; follow State 72 east over Barnegat Bay, and you'll arrive on the island in Ship Bottom at the midpoint. Brant Beach, Beach Haven, and Brighton Beach are to the south, while Barnegat Light, Loveladies, Surf City, and Harvey Cedars are to the north.

20 Holy Flying Chickens, Batman!
Triplebrook Campground, Hope

In the end, it was a chicken by the name of Tiger who won it. Won it big time, she did, flying away from the competition. A big chicken, she was, a Pennsylvania Flyer, according to the kid who'd brought her to the campground. And fly she did, 225 feet by someone's measure, and then roosted high up in a tree, too. We're never going to know how far she'd really have gone if she hadn't lit in that tree. Next best in the contest was the featherweight class winner with the name of Winner, of all things, who managed only twenty-two feet, three inches.

The International Chicken Flying Meet at Triplebrook Campground is just one of the events that attract campers, and sometimes the public, all summer long. People flock (pun intended) to private campgrounds like Triplebrook from all over, seeking the combination of the bucolic setting and friendly social environment.

Private campgrounds are an anomaly, really. They're a mix of summer camp, resort, camping, and the ongoing American love affair with being on the road. People visit for a weekend, a week, or the entire summer. Some purists argue that campground camping is not camping at all, but something more akin to traveling as a self-contained motel. Well, yes, many of the live-in RVs (recreational vehicles) do come equipped with all the amenities of home, and some are literally as big as a small house. While purists may insist that campgrounds are far too cushy, that doesn't preclude purists from camping at commercial campgrounds. Tents are welcome and, if desired, most campgrounds can place you up at a campsite in a beautifully wooded area just far enough from the wash and shower rooms to resemble roughing it.

At Triplebrook, for example, a working 240-acre farm with about 100 acres set aside for camping, the campground contains

200 RV hook-up and tenting sites, many set deep in the woods. If you don't own your own RV but are disinclined to endure the uncertainties of tenting, you can rent a fully equipped air-conditioned trailer.

Beyond the living arrangements, Triplebrook's amenities include two side-by-side swimming pools (one for adults only), a tennis court, a well-stocked country store, a coin laundry, a basketball court, a barnyard full of farm animals, an elaborate model train display, a private lake fully stocked with fish, paddle boats, two plastic kayaks, a RV repair shop, and a lifeguarding staff that doubles as a kiddie camp counseling crew on rainy . . . ("Don't say the 'R' word!" Triplebrook proprietor Brenda James admonishes visitors). Okay then—precipitational days. If that's not enough to keep you occupied, the Jameses print a calendar of the area's special events and nearby recreational options.

Triplebrook, like many campground operations, is a family affair. Operations run by families tend to understand family vacationing needs, especially the need to find a facility that attracts other families so your kids will have other kids to play with. On the that chicken-flying Saturday, the campground overflowed with children. Adults, too, for that matter. Most importantly, everyone was having a good time. During the egg-tossing contest, the two lines of entrants covered enough ground for several first downs in a football game and enough of an age range to qualify for everything from day care to Social Security.

The major problem in picking a campground is deciding on the location that best suits you. According to the New Jersey Campground Owners Association, the state harbors nearly 150 private campgrounds in every kind of setting, from an urban location just fifteen minutes from Times Square, to oceanside, to the mountains, to riverside locales. If you'd like to add a bit of an international flavor to your camping experience, you'll find an enclave of "Nous Parlons Français" campgrounds in the Cape

May area, which for some reason has long been a popular destination for the French-speaking Quebeçois.

Campground camping, by the way, is not limited to summertime. A number of sites offer winter camping, with activities like Nordic skiing, snowmobiling, and ice fishing.

But back to those chickens. If your bird didn't win, you still had a chance to make up for it by making like a chicken yourself. The little kids went ape over the Chicken Scratching Contest, in which they searched with only their toes for Hershey's Kisses scattered on a plastic tarp covered with sawdust. And people seemed willing to make fools of themselves for the Rooster Crowing Contest and the Chicken Legs Chicken Walk Contest. It was as simple as cocka-doodle-doo.

Specifically: Triplebrook (908-459-4079) is located in Hope; reservations are recommended for weekend visitors.

The New Jersey Campground Owners Association offers a free Campground and RV Park Guide; call 609-465-8444, or write to 29 Cook's Beach Road, Cape May Court House, NJ 08210.

21 Living History

The state is alive with the sound of history. The sights, smells, tastes, and feel of it, too. New Jersey provides an abundant opportunity to see everyday life from many time periods recreated and reenacted. Different from restorations or museums, at living history installations you watch artisans at work using the tools of yesteryear and learn about a historic period by talking to people who are "living" it.

Some re-creations are more elaborate than others, but all of them make fascinating time travel.

Allaire State Park, County 524, Farmingdale; 908-938-2371. An 1830s ironworks and mining village, Allaire is also home to the Pine Creek Railroad, where narrow-gauge trains are pulled by historic steam and diesel engines, and to the New Jersey Museum of Transportation. Open daily 8:00 A.M. to 8:00 P.M.

Batsto Historic Village, County 542, Hammonton; 609-561-3262. Another mining community, Batsto was a principal iron source for ammunition production during the Revolution. It was also a glass-making center that thrived from 1766 to 1867. Today, the village is a part of Wharton State Forest, and it contains remnants of a combined industrial and agricultural enterprise dating from the late nineteenth century. The grounds are dominated by Joseph Wharton's mansion, an eerie haunted house–looking building. House tours are given during summer. The original workers' cabins are located across a footbridge from the visitors center and the mansion. There, a small nature center provides information on the local flora and fauna, and a few doors down, a potter and a weaver demonstrate their work. Open daily 8:00 A.M. to 4:30 P.M.

Cold Springs Village, 735 Seashore Road, Cape May; 609-898-2300. Cold Springs is a twenty-building collection that depicts life in a nineteenth-century southern New Jersey farming village. The reception building is decked out in a nautical theme. You sit below deck in a sailing schooner re-creation to watch an orientation video that reviews the history of the Cape May region, tying the sea and agricultural lifestyles together. The "citizens" of Cold Springs Village (from the tinsmith to the schoolmarm) display excellent knowledge of their livelihoods and their roles in village life. Of particular interest is the rope-making demonstration, which utilizes a nifty mechanical device that entwines three lines of hemp. Particularly irresistible are the Village Bakery's goods. Open daily 10:00 A.M. to 4:00 P.M., May to mid-October.

Fosterfields, Kahdena Road and State 24, Morristown; 201-326-7645. Fosterfields takes us to a more recent time—the turn of the twentieth century—to explore life on the farm. Here, visitors are treated to farming the way it was when the Garden State was truly that, including frequent demonstration days (everything from pressing flowers to threshing and harvesting) that illustrate the use of period tools. In addition, the grounds hold a 125-acre arboretum with self-guided trails, including one documented in Braille, and tours of Willows Mansion, a home built by Paul Revere's grandson. Open 10:00 A.M. to 5:00 P.M., Wednesday through Saturday, and 1:00 to 5:00 P.M. Sunday, from April through October.

Howell Living History Farm, Valley Road, Hopewell; 609-737-3299. Howell is another turn-of-the-century working farm, offering a pleasant country hayride in summer and activities almost every weekend throughout the year. Open Tuesday through Saturday 10:00 A.M. to 4:00 P.M., and 12:00 to 4:00 P.M. on Sundays.

Longstreet Farm, Holmdel Park, Longstreet Road, Holmdel; 908-946-3758. Rural life as lived by the Longstreet family during the gay '90s (the 1890s, that is). Open 10:00 A.M. 5:00 P.M. weekdays, 12:00 to 4:30 P.M. weekends.

Millbrook Village, Old Mine Road, Millbrook; 908-496-4458 or 717-588-2451. A highly recommended side trip for anyone exploring the natural beauty of the Delaware Water Gap, Millbrook presents nineteenth-century village life. At its height, Millbrook was home to just seventy-five people, but among the town's current "populace" you'll find a blacksmith, weaver, and several other craftspeople at work. The Garris House tour describes a typical mid-nineteenth-century woman's day. On summer weekends, the town's original gristmill is being re-created, until the project is completed, using period tools. Open from mid-April through Labor Day, 10:00 A.M. to 5:00 P.M.; closed Monday and Tuesday before Memorial Day.

Miller-Cory House, 614 Mountain Avenue, Westfield; 908-232-1776. A 250-year-old farmhouse where eighteenth-century crafts come to life on Sunday afternoons from 2:00 to 5:00 P.M. The house is closed during summer.

New Sweden Farmstead Museum, Bridgeton; 609-451-4802. The City of Bridgeton contains the largest historical district in the state, and third largest in the country (based on the number of buildings). It includes some 2,200 buildings, a 1,100-acre park, four museums, and a zoo. The small, rustic New Sweden Farmstead is located within the park. It depicts a seventeenth-century farmstead typical of those built by Swedish immigrants. Costumed tour guides escort visitors hourly through the bath/smokehouse, threshing barn, blacksmith residence, animal barn, and farmstead home. Open Wednesday through Saturday 11:00 A.M. to 5:00 P.M., and 1:00 to 5:00 P.M. Sundays from mid-April through October; last tour is at 4:00 P.M.

Waterloo Village and Lenape Indian Village, Waterloo Road, Stanhope; 201-347-0900 (see Chapter 28). Waterloo was a main lock station on the Morris Canal, and this is one of the few places where you can see every element of the technology that made that canal an engineering colossus. Home to the New

Jersey Canal Society, the village also offers a close look at small-town life in the early industrial age and, adjacent, a Lenape Indian Village that depicts the region's Native American lifestyle from the time before the Europeans arrived. From April through September, open Tuesday through Sunday 10:00 A.M. to 6:00 P.M.; October through December, closes at 5:00 P.M.

Wheaton Village, 10th and G Streets, Millville; 609-825-6800 (See Chapter 48). Wheaton Village's outstanding Museum of American Glass pays tribute to the artistry of the world's finest glassmakers. The re-created glassworks features demonstrations and antique tools. Crafts and Trades Row presents an opportunity to see many other artisans at work, and the village's Main Street presents the chance to buy their wares. Open daily 10:00 A.M. to 5:00 P.M.; closed Monday and Tuesday during winter (after Christmas).

22 The Sussex Air Show
Sussex

As we drove around the bend, a DC-3 came into view. It sat on the short runway like a majestic bird, the verdant upland hills rising behind it. The workhorse of all airplanes, the DC-3 was the plane that changed the commercial airline business from a bizarre and daring novelty to a viable form of travel. It was also the airplane that did the grit and dirty work of World War II. You don't have to be an airplane buff to appreciate this machine. The plane is unmistakable – its nose sitting high off the ground – and beautiful. And here were not one but three DC-3s parked on the Sussex Airport runway.

Watching the storied past come to life is the essence of the Sussex Air Show, subtitled "The Best Little Air Show in the Country."

Pardon the pun, but from the moment we arrived, we were aware of something special in the air. Folks arrived by car – and by air. One by one, the small planes approached from the south, executed two right turns, and made their final approach with a small mountain rising just behind them. It looked, if you substituted the private planes for television helicopters, like the opening sequence of the TV show "MASH."

Yes, there's the usual "festival" atmosphere found at so many summertime events, but this is different. For one thing, the hot dogs cost $1.50 instead of three bucks; much of the money raised here by admissions and booth sales goes to nonprofit causes; and a sense of amused awe pervades the crowd. They've come, just like folks did sixty years ago, to see if these darned machines really can fly. When the machines do – not only going up and staying up, but flying upside down and in exotic spins or loops – folks are happily amazed. In fact, those Stearman biplanes over there were the same planes that your daddy and granddaddy marvelled at when they left their farming chores and went to gawk at the stunt flying at the air show back in the '30s. They don't call it stunt flying any more, they call it aerobatics, but the pilots must be just as nuts.

The announcer explained the moves and described the action, all the while throwing in good old country-boy humor. Of one flyer he said, "I'd fly with him anytime, anywhere—as long as it wasn't a commercial flight." When two planes took off simultaneously, racing at each other from opposite ends of the runway, he quipped, "I tried to get my sister-in-law to do that; she's got a small car and I tried to pair her up against a big truck." When the "world-renowned" pilot Jimmy Franklin buzzed the runway upside down at an altitude of about six feet, he yelped, "He's flying so low that even the worms will be looking up and ducking their heads!"

Sussex is not a grand military show. No Blue Angels circle the airport. The show evokes the old seat-of-the-pants sensibility. We watched Oscar Boesch swoop his glider down in graceful silence, performing his "sailplane ballet," as the loudspeaker gargled the theme from *Born Free*. We watched befuddled as a tractor-driving "farmer" mowed the grass on the far side of the runway, finally dismounting to bum a ride in a classic Piper Cub, which he promptly "stole," and proceeded to fly in a manner that the small airplane was never designed for.

One thing is significantly different from the old dustbowl barnstorming days. It isn't all boys up there. The Misty Blues, an all-female skydiving team, floated down from the clouds in precise spirals, and a woman calling herself Patty Wagstaff showed why she owned the title National Aerobatics Champion.

The Sussex Air Show is an invention of a guy named Paul Styger. He manages this speck of an aerodrome and first staged this extravaganza some twenty-two years ago. Now, his show not only features three days of fantastic flying, but on the Thursday before the official opening, Styger hosts one of the

Curses, Red Baron!

northeast's largest miniature airplane fly-arounds for model plane enthusiasts.

On show days, arrive early and leave plenty of time to wander among the booths, which sell an enticing variety of goods. Two booths selling model planes were popular with the spectators; T-shirt collections emphasized aircraft and military themes; a variety of aviation-themed art could be purchased; and then there were those DC-3s to admire, antique, handmade, and specially built.

If watching isn't enough for you, and you'd like to experience the old-time thrill of flying in an antique plane, get in touch with an outfit called Bi-Plane Adventures at Old Bridge Airport in Englishtown. Bi-Plane flies, among other craft, a Stearman (circa 1943) and a former Waco cropduster (circa 1940). If you prefer a taste of combat flying, fly-overs in a restored U.S. Navy World War II AT-6 fighter plane can be arranged. Their open cockpit airtours cover New York Harbor and the upper New Jersey shore area, and they'll give you a whole new perspective on flying.

Specifically: The Sussex Air Show takes place annually in late August; call 201-702-9719 or 201-875-7337 for show and scenic flight information. To reach Sussex Airport, take State 23 north into Sussex and turn left onto County 565.

Bi-Plane Adventures flies from April to October. It's best to make a reservation, and they will reschedule if you encounter bad weather. Call 908-446-1300 for information and directions.

23 Artists at Work
Peters Valley Crafts Center, Layton

Peters Valley just might be the ultimate summer camp for crafts-people. They gather at Peters Valley to ply their trade and learn new techniques in ceramics, blacksmithing, fine metalwork, photography, art with fibers, cloth work, woodworking, and jewelry-making by participating in three-day to twelve-day workshops. They work and reside in buildings that include a Greek Revival house, a Dutch Reformed Church, various nine-teenth-century barns, small cottages, and rambling farmhouses. A quiet energy pervades the area, despite the fact that the grounds are spread over many hilly acres.

Indeed, that there are any buildings at all is no small bit of luck. In the late 1960s and early 1970s, the Army Corps of Engineers hatched a plan to dam the nearby Delaware River at a place called Tocks Island. Somewhere between 3,000 and 5,000 buildings were bought and razed before the damming plan was permanently shelved. The area's sparse development bespeaks an era of early rural settlement, so this must be counted among the most bucolic and pleasant settings in New Jersey. Approach-ing over rolling hills and winding roads, the pastoral country-side perfectly sets the mood for viewing the work and workers of Peters Valley.

Your first stop should be the Craft Store and Gallery. Housed in a classic country store complete with covered veranda, this is the Peters Valley nerve center. Inside, works from the various resident student professionals and instructors are tastefully dis-played. The imaginative nature and high quality of the works contrast strongly with the common commercial crafts store fare. Upstairs, the center's gallery offers rotating exhibits, as well as a permanent collection of Peters Valley residents' work. Among the noteworthy gallery events are the Annual Summer Faculty Show and the Annual Studio Assistants' Show.

Come the end of July, in a grassy meadow set on a hill above the Crafts Center and Gallery, Peters Valley mounts arguably the best crafts show in the state. A major fundraising event for the center, the juried show features the work of 150 professional craftspeople representing just about every discipline you can imagine. Music, demonstrations, and excellent food augment the festivities and lend a welcoming air to the informal atmosphere. If you've ever wanted to talk technique with an expert, select from an eclectic range of excellent works, or just find out "how they did that," this is the time and the place. Don't get me wrong. The fair bustles. But it bustles with the kind of appreciative excitement that inspires rather than tires.

Not all of us can schedule our visits around a single weekend's event. Luckily, the Peters Valley studios are open to the public each summer Friday, Saturday, and Sunday afternoon. On a regular weekend, Peters Valley offers a soothing peacefulness. On our latest visit, we arrived at midday on a Sunday. The center was as quiet as a church mouse. We wandered up and down the hills, browsed through the shop and gallery, and snapped photos. Meandering the mown grass path from the parking area to the studios, we enjoyed the hillside's wild, tangled, vegetation, which gave way down below to a brook that bubbled up into a small swamp dotted with luxuriant weeping willows. Across the dirt and gravel drive from the swamp stood a short row of cottages, each personalized in some way with a collection of hanging plants, a postage stamp–sized vegetable garden, or a wicker love seat.

The dirt drive terminated at the ceramics studio. As we approached, an elderly, scraggly dog creakily rose from his rest in a shady spot to greet and inspect us with a creaky wag of his scruffy tail. Two young women stood out front, affably engaged in an intense conversation. The object of their dialogue was a large half-finished piece of clay artwork. We peeked into the long building behind them and found an expansive roomful of ceramicists busily gabbing away over their work. Their creative energy filled the large room, emanating a potent excitement. We were too early, the studio was not yet open to the public, so we slowly turned to stroll back up the road. As we again passed the two women, they had literally taken a step back from the object of their attention, as if to view it neutrally from a distance.

"You see it as a hanging piece, really?" said the creator of the work to her ally. "I see it kind of–drooping down!" They laughed, high-spirited, enjoying the power of creation and the ambiguity of interpretation.

For an artist, the ability to lose one's self in one's work in a calm, focused atmosphere complemented by fellow artists' support is a treasured time. A Peters Valley visit offers the privilege of peeking into their world.

Specifically: Peters Valley Crafts Center (201-948-5200) can be reached from Exit 34 of I-80. Follow State 15 north approximately twenty-six miles; go right onto County 560 west, through the blinking light in the center of Layton, and onto County 640. After approximately one mile, turn right onto County 615 and continue for one mile. Call for a schedule of classes and events.

24 Gardens of the Garden State

The nickname "Garden State" was derived from the "truck farms" – small vegetable farms – that once abounded throughout New Jersey. Although some agriculture survives, a different kind of garden now thrives in the Garden State. We are blessed with some of the most picturesque and pleasant botanical gardens, arboretums, and formal public gardens to be found anywhere.

Here are just three I particularly like, one south, one mid-state, and one north:

Leaming's Run
Cape May Court House
A woman sat at a wooden table, half hidden behind a pile of dried flowers and baskets that she was turning into artful arrangements. She hummed as she worked and smiled graciously as she took my entrance fee.

"Do you have a brochure or guide to the gardens?" I asked. She shook her head. "Just follow the path."

Like follow the yellow brick road? Well, yes, there's a bit of Oz in Leaming's Run. The dirt path winds through the woods, connecting a series of clearings that reveal magnificent, colorful tableaux. The largest annual-flower garden in the United States, Leaming's Run covers some thirty acres and holds twenty-five small gardens, each planted with a theme. A small sign explains each garden's composition and plants. Periodically, and delightfully, you come upon a sign that says, "Look Back!" reminding you that sometimes beauty is waiting just behind you.

After passing through the Yellow, Blue and White, and English Cottage Gardens, I encountered a Swedish Colonial Farmstead, with a one-room log cabin, circa 1695. As I entered, a mother and daughter were fussing over a peacock that lolled in a deep, dusty hole it had dug. The women, camera at the ready, were trying to coax it out to show its feathers. Like a somnambulant cat, it disdained their attentions. Cameras are a must at Leaming's Run. The individual mini-vistas demand photographing, especially when you come to the Begonia Garden, Gazebo Garden, and Bridal Garden, all centered on a classic streamside gazebo and a nearby footbridge. At path's end, the Cooperage Gift Shop sells pretty and reasonably priced dried flower arrangements and a book entitled "Gardening Without Work" by Jack Aprill, the man who is behind all this beauty.

Frelinghuysen Arboretum
Morristown

The oompah band was gathering on the portable stage, a crowd was gathering on the expansive lawn below the mansion house, and an ominous collection of thunderheads was gathering overhead. Did we have time to wander among the flowers and trees, and could the band commence playing before the rain commenced falling?

Over 125 acres, the Frelinghuysen Arboretum displays a unique collection of trees, flowers, and shrubs in an easily accessed, well-annotated fashion. The Haggerty Education Center offers a variety of horticultural learning opportunities for all ages, year-round, and includes a library, changing exhibits, and an engaging display of carriages from the late nineteenth and early twentieth centuries.

We opted to follow the "Blue Trail," which seemed long enough to provide some mild exercise and short enough to allow us to sit through part of the concert and/or retreat from the impending storm. We were rewarded with an extremely pleasant walk through a variety of plants and terrain on a trail that was very clearly marked and well-supported by the guide. From Chinese Stranvaesia (an evergreen ground cover) to Hardy

Rubber Trees and a detour through a wet meadow rich with wild grasses, the Blue Trail revealed a rich variety of flora. About halfway through our walk, just as sounds of the band drifted over the hill, the clouds dissipated. Now, we could stroll to a musical accompaniment under sunny skies.

The Blue Trail reascended the hill in front of the white Colonial Revival–style mansion house, but we diverted into the Knot Garden, a garden of English Tudor origin. A brick path and a pond beautifully surrounded by large, white-flowering Japanese snowbell and oakleaf hydrangea proved just too tempting. We sat here on a bench and let the band's pops sound float above us, completing a classic, lazy summer Sunday afternoon.

Ringwood Manor State Park
Ringwood
Skylands and Ringwood Manor together transport you back to a genteel time – long before air conditioning – when gentlemen and ladies lolled the summer away on estates where the cooler high-country weather provided much-needed relief from the city's heat.

An investment banker and trustee of the New York Botanical Garden, Clarence McKenzie Lewis set out in 1922 to create a botanical showplace at Skylands. He built a magnificent Tudor-style mansion made of native granite and rich woods, then had the most prominent landscape architects design a suitable setting for the extensive collection of plants he had gathered from around the world. The state of New Jersey purchased the property in 1966 and declared it the official State Botanical Garden in 1984.

Today, Skylands offers visitors a serene escape from the hectic megalopolis just half an hour's drive away. The house is not open to the public, so you'll have to content yourself with admiring it from the outside, but you can pick up a self-guided tour brochure at the carriage house.

Maple Avenue, the main road, is paralleled on the left by two lines of Carmine crab apple trees that stretch for an impressive 1,600 feet through an expansive lawn called Swan Meadow. In front of these are the Annual and Perennial Gardens. Behind, to the east, several interweaving footpaths lead you to informal displays of rhododendron, heather, and wildflowers. Continue back into the heavily wooded area at the base of a wooded hill called Mount Defiance and you find a bog garden and, eventually, the picturesque Swan Pond.

Westward, across Maple Avenue, are the formal gardens. Leaving the house's rear terrace, you come upon an octagonal pool surrounded by dwarf plants and evergreen shrubs from a variety of places. Next comes the Magnolia Walk, two parallel lines of southern sweet bay magnolias, planted where their fragrance could drift up to the nearby house. That's followed by the Azalea Garden, a rectangular reflecting pool lined by azaleas and rhododendrons of almost every conceivable color. Immediately below the azaleas, the Summer Garden features day lilies. Next, you'll come to a collection of tree peonies that borders the Lilac Garden. Come May, Skylands' collection of nearly 400 lilac varieties presents an array that nearly overwhelms the eye.

It's but a short drive to Ringwood Manor. The first section of the manor was built in 1765, and the building, having been purchased by the iron-magnate Hewitt family in 1807, was expanded section by section for many years. The final structure includes seventy-eight rooms. The building is filled with marvelous paraphernalia dating from the early 1800s to the mid-1900s, and the free manor tour is well-conducted. The Manor also houses a small art gallery and magnificent formal gardens of its own.

Also a short drive within the state park is Shepherd's Lake, an oversized pond, really. The lake area has a snack bar and swimming, small boating, fishing, and picnicking are permitted.

Specifically: The New Jersey Division of Travel and Tourism's Outdoor Guide lists many of the state's formal gardens and arboretums; call 1-800-537-7397 to obtain a copy.

Leaming's Run Gardens (609-465-5871) is on US 9 north of Cape May; take the Garden State Parkway to Exit 13, go west on Avalon Boulevard and north on US 9. Open from May through October, with special hummingbird tours in August.

The Frelinghuysen Arboretum (201-736-7600) is located at 53 East Hanover Avenue in Morristown. From I-287 northbound, take Exit 36A, proceed to Whippany Road, turn right onto East Hanover Avenue at the second light. From I-287 southbound, take Exit 36, turn right onto Ridgedale Avenue and right at the first traffic light onto East Hanover Avenue.

Skylands Botanical Gardens of Ringwood State Park (201-962-7031 or 201-962-7527) and Ringwood Manor (201-962-9534 for recorded event information) are located off County 511. From I-80, take State 23 north to Butler, exit onto County 511 north and go about fifteen miles, following the signs.

25 A Retreat Treat
Ocean Grove

Question: What do Teddy Roosevelt, New Jersey governor Christie Whitman, John Philip Sousa, Glen Miller, Ulysses S. Grant, Guy Lombardo, Booker T. Washington, Jascha Heifitz, Billy Graham, Woodrow Wilson, and The Preservation Hall Jazz Band all have in common?

Answer: They've all graced the stage – to speak or perform – of the Great Auditorium in Ocean Grove.

Built in 1894, the magnificent hall remains Ocean Grove's centerpiece. Visitors still flock to hear speakers and concerts of all kinds and to attend religious services. Regardless of the event or occasion, the building itself is transfixing. It is, according to Larry Jackson, CEO of the Ocean Grove Camp Meeting Association, the largest all-wood auditorium in the country, covering nearly the length of a football field, seating 6,400 people, and housing an enormous Robert Hope Jones pipe organ. The roof is made of long, arched wooden planks and is said to have been conceived as Noah's ark, upside down. That's impressive. But when you learn that it was built in ninety-two days by sixty workers (and that the workers swore an oath not to drink, smoke, or curse while working on the construction), impressive turns into awesome.

Indeed, much about Ocean Grove is awesome. And curious. The town was founded in 1869 as a religious retreat for the Methodist Episcopal Church. It was not uncommon in those days for believers who sought spiritual uplifting, as well as relief from their daily cares and the summer's heat, to gather together, live in tents for several days or even weeks at a time, and listen to inspiring sermons and music. They called these gatherings Camp Meetings. Ocean Grove's Camp Meeting Association represents one of the nation's two longest continually operating camp meeting organizations. The faithful no longer pitch tents, however. They set up the canvases over wooden platforms; there are 114 of them available. The canvas areas serve as the small homes' front rooms; diminutive wood cabins, equipped with electricity, bathrooms, and kitchens, attach to the rear of the platforms.

Today's tents offer more comforts of home than their predecessors, but the spirit that founded the town has not weakened. Weekly concerts are performed on the magnificent auditorium pipe organ, guest clerics from around the country lead Sunday morning services, the Tabernacle Bible Hour meets every weekday at 9:00 A.M., and the mid-July camp meeting week still highlights the summer.

Time was when local blue laws closed the town off to worldly pleasures every Saturday at midnight. In fact, a chain blocked the road at the town's entry gates, and no wheeled vehicles were permitted to even be seen (no less operated) for twenty-four hours. But Ocean Grove today can't be characterized as all religion and no fun. Yes, it remains a dry town, and the public bathhouse doesn't open until afternoon on Sundays, but the engaging downtown is inviting and as active as any at the shore. Quaint galleries, singular gift shops, and several restaurants create an enjoyable browsing and strolling atmosphere. Try lunch at the Sampler Inn, which serves very affordable meals in an old-fashioned cafeteria style.

As might be expected, Ocean Grove's boardwalk offers oceanfront serenity, not action. On the beach, volleyball tournaments, kite-flying contests, water races, and sand sculpture contests take place throughout the summer. The town's annual events include a December Festival of Lights and the Holiday House Tour, the November Harvest Home Festival, and an Oktoberfest.

Those who crave nightlife need drive but ten minutes north, however, to find one of the Garden State's most famous

The tent city at Ocean Grove

nightspots – Asbury Park's Stone Pony, which gave Bruce Springsteen his start. Next door, The Hitching Rail, a nightspot that's quickly growing in popularity, features country music. Asbury Park has long been famous for offering evenings chock full of the classic boardwalk cacophony of games, rides, and bright lights.

Ocean Grove's Victorian-rich architecture and religious-retreat orientation combine to create a unique character. The little seaside town has been placed on the National Register of Historic Places, and it represents, Larry Jackson is quick to point out, "The largest assemblage of Victorian architecture in an area of this size." While Ocean Grove's Victorian flavor feels a bit rough around the edges and hasn't attained the fame or the panache of Cape May, its collection of seaside hotels, bed and breakfasts, and inns offer a beach holiday in the old style that spans several eras. The Lilligard, for example, is a small hotel that has operated since 1871.

Still, it's the summer auditorium concerts that bring the most attention to Ocean Grove, and rightfully so. There is nothing ostentatious or overly ornate about the building – its only somewhat garish features are the three church-like steeples at its front. Yet this is clearly a special space, one with acoustics that resound with every nuance of projected sound. It bestows a special pride to the performers, preachers, and even the local children's theater club members who grace its stage – a stage that contributes both identity and faith to an entire community.

Specifically: To reach Ocean Grove from the north or west, take the Garden State Parkway to Exit 100-B or the New Jersey Turnpike to Exit 8 and follow State 33 west; from the south, take the Turnpike to I-195 east to State 35 north.

For general and event information, call 1-800-388-4768, or call the Camp Meeting Association at 908-775-0035.

26 Cabin Camping

Our tent is jinxed. Every time we pitch it, we're flooded out. We've spent most of our tenting trips at the laundromat running sleeping bags through the dryer.

Face it. When it comes to camping, we're not troopers.

That's why when cousin Vera asked us to join her family for camping, we hesitated. Vera had two kids at the time – girls whose ages were young and very young. The idea of suffering through a deluge with infants was daunting. Our own kids were seven and nine, and they already hated tenting because of the unfailing torrential rains.

"This will be different," cousin Vera assured us. "We'll rent a family cabin. You can do that at a lot of state parks." Rent a cabin? We remained skeptical, but Vera talked us into it. Two months later, as we drove to the mountains, we could only imagine the worst. We envisioned a dirty collection of rotting boards with a squeaky screen door and a musty reek that leaned precariously, ready to collapse with the first hard (and inevitable) rain. It probably had a dank privy out back.

We were right about the screen door squeaking, but we were wrong about the rest. The cabin was an immaculately clean, roomy building made of sweet-smelling, rough-hewn pine, and it was downright comfortable. A path through the trees led to the lake just a few yards away, where we fished, hiked, and skipped stones. Small, electric motor–powered boats and canoes were available for rent, too.

The kids went ga-ga over fishing. The girls loved dangling their lines from the shore. Many small fish were snagged; all were thrown back – except one, and he was the biggest we caught. The poor guy swallowed the hook and died. Not knowing what else to do with him, we tossed him on a rock next to a waiting water snake, then spent fifteen minutes in rapt fascination watching that skinny snake ingest that fat fish. No science class will ever make a stronger impression on those kids.

Yes, it rained on that camping trip. We didn't care. We had a real roof over our heads. We stayed dry.

We've become big fans of cabin camping. You get some of the comforts of home, some of the rough edges of camping, no backaches from sleeping on the ground, and never a wet sleeping bag.

A number of New Jersey state parks offer cabin camping. Most have bunks beds, cold running water, kitchen facilities complete with refrigerator and stove, and flush toilets. Sizes range from four bunks to twenty-four bunks. You must bring your own linens or sleeping bags, kitchen utensils, and towels. Cabins can be rented by the week or by the weekend. As you would expect, in the heart of summer, rentals are very popular, and reservations are a must—the further ahead, the better.

Up north, Stokes State Forest and nearby High Point are the places to cabin camp. Although both offer launch sites for small boats, neither of these parks provides rowboat or canoe rentals.

Toward the state's center, Wharton, Lebanon, and Parvin State Forests offer cabin camping. Wharton and Parvin also have small-boat rental. A family trip to Wharton State Forest can combine a fantastic variety of activities—hiking, fishing, canoeing, mountain or road biking, and a living history visit to Batsto Village—for a very reasonable price without the usual discomforts of tent camping.

Farther south, Bass River, along the south central shore, and Belleplain, north of Dennisville, are the cabin camping sites, and both offer great access to lake and river canoeing.

Incidentally—all these beautiful parks and forests offer tent camping, as well, some with true wilderness campsites. You'll find plenty of places to pitch a tent. Just don't ask to borrow ours unless you like tenting in the rain.

Specifically: The Department of Environmental Protection, Division of Parks and Forestry offers information on all state parks and forests, including a fee schedule for all park activities. They've divided the state into three regions, south, central, and north. Contact the Region One office in Hammonton at 609-965-5220, the Region Two Freehold office at 908-462-5868, and the Region Three office in Franklin at 201-827-6200; or call the state office at 609-292-2797. To write for information: New Jersey Department of Environmental Protection, Division of Parks and Forestry, CN 404, Trenton, NJ 08625.

27 Horse Country
Cream Ridge and Allentown

Verdant and replete with gently rolling meadows, hills, and woodlands, Cream Ridge is home to a handful of very special horse farms. Residing in the barns and playing in the fields of these farms are some of the greatest standardbred horses that ever ran – or trotted – a race.

If you're like me and don't know a standardbred from a nag, here's the scoop: standardbreds are the horses that compete in harness racing, as opposed to thoroughbreds, which run at a full gallop. Harness racers are divided into trotters and pacers, the difference being their racing gait. Standardbreds and thoroughbreds also differ in their breeding. (And with racehorses, breeding is of the utmost importance.) Standardbreds may be bred through artificial insemination. Thoroughbreds may not.

I learned all this at Walnridge Farm. Dr. David Meirs II, veterinarian and founder of the Walnridge equine breeding program, is proud to show off his prize horses and to talk about the farm that he converted in 1972 from an unsuccessful dairy operation to standardbred breeding predominance.

"The farm has been in the family since 1830," Dr. Meirs told me as we admired the stallions. "We began breeding when the New Jersey Sire Stakes program was instituted. That's a program in which New Jersey harness tracks sponsor a series of races only for horses conceived in New Jersey."

Conceived, that's the important word. A competing horse can live anywhere, but impregnation has to have taken place in the Garden State. Keeping in mind that, for racehorses, lineage is vital, and that artificial insemination is acceptable for standardbreds, the importance of the Sire Stakes program becomes obvious – bring your mare to one of these Monmouth County farms, home to the best of the best, have her impregnated here, and the offspring qualify to return to New Jersey to win big money.

We entered a large, rather barren, square room with concrete floors and noticed a large object at one side. It looked like an oversized gymnastic pommel horse that had a hollow section and was laden with several contraption-like attachments. "This is an artificial vagina," Dr. Meirs elucidated. "We train the stallions to use it, and then the semen is put into cold storage until it's inseminated into the mares. With artificial insemination, we can fertilize twenty mares a day." The doctor smiled. "There's very little romance involved. We refer to it as drive-by breeding."

Four major standardbred farms are located in the Cream Ridge area, attracting mares from around the world. At Walnridge alone, as many as a thousand horses–mares, foals, stallions, and yearlings–will be in residence at any time during the year.

Walnridge's barns bring you face to face with some of the most successful harness-racing horses of all time. In residence here, among others, are Presidential Ball, a $3 million winner; Beach Towel, the 1990 World Champion; and Niatross, winner of thirty-seven of his thirty-nine races, world speed record setter, and harness-racing triple crown winner. They're all studs now, and they live a pretty good life, with 315 acres in which to run. It makes the concept of being retired to stud rather appealing.

Horse Park of New Jersey

A short distance from the breeding grounds of Cream Ridge, along I-195, the Horse Park of New Jersey operates as a nonprofit, volunteer-run, educational facility. Founded by state agencies and a consortium of horse industry groups, the site has been developed into a premier equine showplace.

The park contains two large show rings, one of which is equipped with lights for nighttime events. In addition, a grass schooling ring and a fenced outside course are used for training and various events.

The Horse Park hosts weekend activities from March through November, including a number of riding events for people with disabilities. The facility houses twin mounting ramps designed to help the physically challenged to ride.

You can also go to auctions at the Horse Park. Standardbred sales are carried on here periodically.

More is in the offing. Hunt and grand prix courses are planned in adjacent fields, and a new Equine Building will house winter shows.

You can't hire a horse here or come to the Horse Park for recreational riding, but for anyone who enjoys watching horses in action, as showplaces go, this facility stands with the best of them.

Downtown Allentown

After cavorting with the equines, pay a visit to Allentown — a classic one-horse town.

The village was founded in 1706 when Nathan Allen set up a mill next to Doctor's Creek. The mill still stands, but it no longer grinds grains. It now houses a delightful German restaurant, the Black Forest, and a trio of crafts shops. Thick, rough-hewn beams and posts, a rough stucco finish on the walls, and the original woodwork around the windows create a rustically genial atmosphere. Be sure to take a trip to the restrooms. After winding down the broad board stairs, you emerge into a dungeon-like cellar. The route to the lavatories passes ancient wooden gears, mill wheels, and grinding stones that lie about like items in any home basement — as if they're just waiting for

Mr. Homeowner to get them up and running on his next free Saturday.

For more usable antiques, The Country Corner Antiques, established next door to the mill in a three-story colonial house, offers a high-quality and varied collection. Then run across the street to The Stitchery, an old-fashioned shop filled with treasures and trash.

Specifically: Walnridge Farm (609-758-8208) is located on Arneytown-Hornerstown Road. Call for the best visiting times and specific directions.

The Horse Park of New Jersey (609-259-0170) is located just off Exit 11 of I-195.

To reach Allentown, exit I-195 onto County 526 (Red Valley Road) and follow it south.

28 A Unique Music Mix
Waterloo Village, Stanhope

Some places lend themselves well to imaginative conjecture. On a splendid summer's eve, sitting outside the performance tent at Waterloo Village, I can't resist pondering what the good folks from the eighteenth-century Allen and Turner Company would think about their state-of-the-art industrial town having become a summertime center for celebrating the musical arts.

Prior to the Revolution, Allen and Turner, a Philadelphia company, developed this spot into an iron-processing center, taking advantage of vast ore deposits in the nearby hills and the built-in power provided by the Musconetcong River. The ironworks flourished. Mills were established. The new community, named Andover Forge in honor of Turner's birthplace in England, prospered, and the company built large homes for its forge foreman and ironmaster to celebrate their success.

After the war, although the area had been denuded of the timber that fueled the works, a family named Smith took over operations and expanded into a range of commercial agricultural endeavors. Brig. Gen. John Smith reestablished the ironworks and, in 1815, he renamed the foundry, Waterloo Foundry, to celebrate the defeat of Napoleon. The new name stuck, and soon the whole town was known as Waterloo.

Waterloo's approaching heyday was to prove bittersweet. The pivotal time was 1863; the event, the completion of the 102-mile Morris Canal, an engineering marvel that ran from Phillipsburg to Jersey City. The sweetness lay in Waterloo's key location along the canal; a lot of coal passed through the Waterloo lock, and the town's importance as an inland "port" brought unprecedented prosperity. The bitter pill? The coming of the railroads. By the turn of the century, the rails replaced the waterway and Waterloo was bypassed altogether. The village was knocked from its commercially prominent perch.

Today, Waterloo Village functions as a historical restoration within Allamuchy State Park (see Chapter 21). The restoration is unique because it also contains each major engineered element of the historic canal, including a lock and an inclined plane. The latter was an ingenious invention of Robert Fulton's that used waterpower and short stretches of railroad track to move boats to high or low canal sections. A visit to Waterloo's Canal Museum explains all this and more.

But Waterloo is best known for its dedication to the arts. Visitors can view visual art, attend antique and craft shows, participate in an Oktoberfest or a handful of ethnic festivals, and enjoy professional dance performances or the annual Geraldine R. Dodge Poetry Festival. Even with all that to choose from, it's music that sets Waterloo apart, as we found out one hot summer's day.

Traffic came to a complete stop. Cars were backed up for miles, and no progress in sight. But nobody minded. I had a minivan full of thirteen-year-old boys and enough picnic stock to last a month. When we came to a standstill, we just opened the sliding door, popped the rear hatch, and feasted until traffic began to move.

We were headed to Waterloo Village for an event called Lollapalooza. Lollapalooza is a the closest thing that today's rock 'n roll generation has to Woodstock, and that includes the haplessly commercial Woodstock revival of '94. A raucous and exuberant traveling festival, complete with two stages and dozens of booths selling jewelry, trinkets, clothes, incense, and food, the tour has quickly become an icon for young "alternative rock" lovers and gained a reputation as the place where such bands as Pearl Jam got their big break.

By the time we'd been funneled through the gate to Waterloo's concert field, my charges were psyched beyond belief.

The water-powered gristmill at Waterloo Village

Through the sweltering summer afternoon and well into the night, they ran wild-eyed through the crowds, jumped to music played at fearful decibel levels, and generally celebrated their own youth.

Me? I drank it all in like a thirsty dog who has stumbled upon a large lake, frequently musing on the historical irony: heavy-metal rock was wafting over the heavy-industrial processing center of centuries past.

Not all Waterloo music caters to the teenage set. Indeed, most speaks to the finer elements. You can bask in Bach, Beethoven, or Mahler; listen to jazz greats; and tap your toe to some of the best banjo pickin' this side of Tennessee. In the future, Waterloo will be the summer home of the Metropolitan Opera. Musical events here cover such a wide range of styles that everyone of every taste will find something to like.

Waterloo Village is one of four stops on the Skylands Trail of Historical Sites. The other three are: Historical Speedwell Village near Morristown, the birthplace of steamship engines and the electromagnetic telegraph; Oxford Furnace/Shippen Manor, site of America's first heated-air blast furnace; and Sterling Mine and Museum, the last working zinc mine in the state, and a site that contains more than 300 minerals, seventy of them fluorescent. In combination, they provide insight into how the Industrial Revolution came to fruition in this country.

Specifically: Waterloo Village (201-347-0900) operates from mid-April to Christmas. Take I-80 to US 206 north and follow the signs.

29 Crafts, Football, and Shakespeare
Madison

> "O! it is excellent
> To have a giant's strength, but it's tyrannous
> To use it like a giant."
>
> —William Shakespeare
> *Measure for Measure*, Act II, Scene II

Madison is at once likable and unremarkable. Its small downtown has a comfortable feel, the shops being neither too posh nor too tawdry. In midsummer, however, unremarkable Madison offers a quietly remarkable combination of crafts, arts, and sports.

At the heart of town sits the Museum of Early Trades and Crafts, a small and too-little-known gem. The museum is set in the remarkable James Library Building, built at the turn of the century in the Romanesque Revival style to create, according to an 1899 newspaper report, "a building quiet in effect, rather than gaudy" (befitting a library's purpose). The museum houses permanent and special exhibits dedicated to "preserving the lives and works of the craftsmen, farmers, and homemakers that shaped New Jersey's preindustrial society." Of particular interest is the exhibit entitled "Children of the Eighteenth and Nineteenth Centuries." Much mention is made of proper training and education.

Just outside downtown Madison lie three college campuses. At Fairleigh Dickinson University (FDU), the New York Football Giants gather from mid-July until mid-August. You can't get a ticket to see the Giants during the regular season (unless, of course, you've inherited season tickets, or have a connection), and their in-season practices are closed to the public. But here at FDU, in an estate-like setting of tree-lined lanes and stone bridges, two practices a day are open for all to see.

Don't get me wrong. Coming to a training camp practice does not equate to watching a game at Giants Stadium. There's no pomp, no circumstance, and the only electricity in the air comes from petulant thunderstorms. So what do you get? A chance to watch the Boys of Autumn up close and personal; a chance to appreciate the physical enormity of these men, their incredible agility, stature, and grace; and an opportunity, perhaps, to bear witness to the seeds of greatness – you never know in July whether you might be watching the next Super Bowl champions.

The first time I brought my son Dan to training camp, he watched wide-eyed. Later, he was able to talk, even if just for a moment, with several of the players, and he easily collected the autographs kids so dearly desire. Try doing that in November. The atmosphere among the spectators is relaxed and enthusiastic. Picnic lunches are as plentiful as the critical evaluations of this year's prospects. The players carry out their drills with diligence, but clearly show rough edges. It's much like witnessing a great play in rehearsal. Six months after my initial training camp visit, the team dominated Denver in the Super Bowl. They'd "strutted and fretted their hour upon the stage" and they were a hit – world champs. I'd seen them at the formative stages and was able to appreciate how far they'd come.

Just a few miles down the road from the FDU practice fields, you'll find the Drew University campus. Here, instead of tree-lined lanes, you find footpaths set under a thick, forest-like canopy, and another kind of team struts and frets their hour upon the stage. After more than thirty years of performing as New Jersey's only classical theater, the New Jersey Shakespeare Festival has begun to gain national prominence. This is first-rate theatre, performed by an Equity (actor's union) troupe and supported by experienced designers and directors. The Who's Who in the cast lists artists with experience on Broadway, Off-

Broadway, at major regional theaters, and in television and film.

The festival currently takes place in Drew University's Bowne Theater, which was originally a gymnasium and is now a comfortable and charismatic little theater. A new facility will be built in the near future, but Bowne is really a great place to watch a play—large enough to allow some spectacle, small enough to lend an intimate feeling. Arriving early, you can purchase a soft drink from the rolling cart positioned outside the theater's front door, stroll the campus grounds, or picnic at the tables on the grass nearby.

The company shows a lively willingness to experiment, often responding to the classics with imagination and creative interpretation. The 1994 season, for example, included a production of *The Merry Wives of Windsor* set in the 1950s at a Catskills resort. The result was a fast-paced, clever show that simultaneously bridged the gap between the distant past (Elizabethan England) and modernity (1950s America) while enhancing the audience's appreciation by taking it on a nostalgia trip into its own past.

In addition to Shakespeare, the summer line-up of plays might include the Greek classics, while modern classics are performed by the troupe's Other Stage company at the Playwright's Theater in downtown Madison. A "Monday Night at the Movies" series complements the stage offerings, providing, for example, an opportunity to see *Romeo and Juliet* on stage during the weekend followed by the great Franco Zeffirelli film interpretation of the play on Monday evening.

Summertime Madison really does become the little town of giants. Take Mr. Shakespeare up on this invitation, and . . .

"You sunburnt gentlemen of August weary,
Come hither from the furrow and be merry."
The Tempest, Act IV, Scene I

Specifically: To reach Madison, take I-78 to State 24 west, or I-287 to State 24 east. When you reach town, the museum is on the right on Main Street; follow the signs to the colleges.

The Museum of Early Trades and Crafts (201-377-2982) is open Tuesday through Saturday from 10:00 A.M. to 4:00 P.M., and from 2:00 to 5:00 P.M. on Sundays. Call for a special exhibits and events calendar.

The Giants' practice schedule varies. Call the team's main Giants Stadium offices at 201-935-8111 for information and directions to the FDU campus.

The New Jersey Shakespeare Festival (201-408-5600) season runs from mid-May through Labor Day. Main stage performances take place on Tuesday through Sunday evenings, and matinees are presented on Wednesday, Saturday, and Sunday. The Other Stage performs on Tuesday through Saturday evenings and on Saturday afternoon. "Monday Night at The Movies" usually begins at 8:00 P.M.

The festival office can recommend theater and lodging and/or dining packages.

30 Balloon Magic
Pittstown

Awesome. There's no other word for these color-bursting, lighter-than-air flying machines we call hot air balloons. They rise from the ground like sleeping giants coming slowly awake. When, over the course of perhaps half an hour, seventy-five or more balloons stand tall and rise, they change the landscape. What was a remote clearing in the woods has become something akin to a lollipop jungle as thickly overgrown as the Amazon. Only here, the lollipops stand sixty to 120 feet high. And they can fly.

The Magic of Alexandria Hot Air Balloon Festival turns a tiny private airfield into a hotbed of activity each year during the first weekend of August. The central activities begin in mid-afternoon when Santa Claus and two of his helpers make a surprising off-season visit, arriving not by airborne reindeer-pulled sled, but via sky-diving parachutes from a height of 3,000 feet. The brightly colored chutes loop to the ground like oversized seed pods with humans dangling beneath them, presenting a glimpse of the eye-dazzling airborne hues to come.

Shortly thereafter begins the parade of balloonists. Led onto the runway by a Marine bagpipe band and the local fire company's trucks—lights flashing and sirens blaring—the balloon pilots and their support teams pass before the enthusiastic crowd, then circle around to begin inflation. One by one the balloons fill out like flowers opening to the sun. The familiar teardrop shapes are so resplendent one is hard-pressed to know where to look first, or which looks best. The shiny nylon fabric makes the most of the fluorescent greens, deep purples, and fireball oranges and reds. When each new color combination reaches the sky, it instantly becomes your new favorite.

But then the special shapes arise. Mickey Mouse. A moving truck. A giant sneaker. Enough "Ooohs" and "Ahhs" fill the air

114

to match the clatter of the enormous fans that force the air into the balloons and the fiery whoosh of the propane tanks that heat the canopies and send them aloft. Up they go. Like a flock, the balloons rise and drift downwind toward the horizon until the sky resembles a flying polkadot circus. And then they're gone. But never fear, they'll soon be back for the "balloon glow." In the meantime, there are 250 country fair–style booths to explore, trampolines to bounce on, a climbing wall to ascend, flight simulators in which to play pilot, assorted games to play, music to hear, and tons of food to eat. A special "Hang Out Hangar" offers amusement just for the little ones, while the beer garden and the Garden State Wine Growers wine garden allow adults to relax with a refreshing "adult beverage." All the while, a small airforce of single-engine planes and a pair of helicopters are taking off and landing, offering eighteen-minute rides for a fee, and skydivers keep falling from the sky. Actually, a number of skydivers rise into the sky. They drive "paraplanes," a contraption that combines a skydiver's chute rigged up to a go-cart-like frame, with a large rear-mounted engine and fan that propels the driver at twenty-six miles per hour.

I don't know about you, but I'll never look at a hot air balloon rising, its basket dangling below, without thinking of Dorothy left forlornly behind by the erstwhile Wizard of Oz. At the Alexandria Airfield, however, you needn't be left standing on the ground. Just buy a ride. They're not cheap, but if you've never experienced the serenity of silently riding on the wind, it's well worth it.

Each evening of the festival centers around a different theme. The Friday night theme during our visit was "The Magic of Country," featuring a kids' play, a country music band, and a western stage show in the entertainment tent. That Saturday was all about "Flights of Fantasy – a Celebration of 200 Years of Ballooning," and the Sunday theme was "Fantasy Faces," complete with a celebrity faces stage show, a swimsuit fashion show, and stunt flying.

Come dusk, the balloonists reappear and reinflate on the runway infield. Staying tethered to the ground, on the count of ten all the pilots fire their propane burners, and the field is ablaze with iridescent glowing jewels. They call this the "balloon glow." Eye dazzling, to say the least. I don't know that I've ever seen anything quite like it. A fireworks finale followed. The fireworks are fine, but the glow left me with an everlasting imprint.

To top off the good feeling, it's nice to know that part of the festival's earnings are donated to charity; in recent years the beneficiary has been the Make-A-Wish Foundation.

New Jersey offers two annual festivals. Oddly, they are staged a mere week apart. The New Jersey Festival of Ballooning takes place in Readington a week before Magic of Alexandria, which means balloon enthusiasts can double their pleasure.

Specifically: The Magic of Alexandria Hot Air Balloon Festival (908-735-0870) is held during the first full weekend of August at the Alexandria Field Airport in Pittstown. Admission is charged. To get to the airport, take I-78 to Exit 12 and follow County 625 south. Cross over County 579 and continue south to Airport Road and turn right. Coming from the south, take US 202 north to State 12 west to County 579 north. Turn left onto County 625 to Airport Road, and turn right.

The New Jersey Festival of Ballooning (908-534-4000) takes place at the end of July at the Solberg-Hunterdon County Airport in Readington. Admission is charged. Call for directions.

31 The Scandinavian Fest
Budd Lake

In the end, it was the Swedish pancakes that proved an irresistible lure.

"Ooooh-oooh," cooed Leena as she read the brochure. "Swedish pancakes! I haven't had those in a long time. They're goooood!"

We figured that Leena (pronounced Lay-na) knew from whence she spoke. She's a Finnish emigree; she should know about things Scandinavian. And so, on Labor Day Sunday (what I'd call the unofficial first day of autumn), in search of Swedish pancakes, we piled into the van for the trip to Budd Lake's Vasa Park, site of the 10th Annual Scandinavian Fest.

You should've seen the line at the pancake house!

Of a seemingly endless number of ethnic festivals in New Jersey, this one stands out. Sponsored by two member lodges of the Vasa Order of America, a Scandinavian cultural and fraternal order, the fair's producers have gone to great lengths to keep the event as homespun and "pure" as possible.

"A lot of these ethnic festivals present anything that is remotely connected with the nationality," Carl Anderson, Vasa Fest organizer, told me on the phone. "At an Italian festival, you'll get some guy named Smith singing songs that Frank

Sinatra made famous. But we try to make sure this event truly reflects the culture and crafts of Scandinavia."

Just for the record, Scandinavia includes Denmark, Finland, Iceland (betcha didn't know that), Norway, and Sweden. As far as I could tell, the fair met Mr. Anderson's assessment. Yes, the requisite hot dog and pizza booths were available, but the prevailing tenor was to homemade and decidedly ethnic goods and foods, and many people showed up dressed in traditional costumes.

The food proved especially interesting, with booths mounted by both professional purveyors and Vasa lodges. How about some limpa cardamon, a pastry-like dish available at the Nordic Imports and Bakery booth? Or leverposte, Danish meat cakes with aster (cucumber) and beets from the Scandia Deli? Even this vegetarian was tempted by the kaldolmar och inglada gurkor (translation: stuffed cabbage and pickled cucumbers) offered by the Draken Lodge #731 of the Vasa of America. Leena loyally opted for a plate of Finnish salmon sandwiches and karelianpi, a kind of rye dough and potato pastry. Her namesake, our daughter Laina, went directly to a stand called Big Olaf of Bergen to indulge in a triple scoop waffle ice cream cone, made with a freshly baked-before-your-eyes waffle.

The craft and gift booths, too, reflected a true homeland spirit. Yes, you could purchase your official Fest T-shirt, or one that proclaimed "Leif Landed First!" But you could also purchase handmade wooden carvings from the German Hill Farm collection of Celtic and Nordic folklore, a Norwegian stove from SOS Stoves & Fireplaces, wood items from Tomten's Workshop, and wooden handicrafts from Bengtsson och Pettersson. My favorite item was found at the Nordic Gallery – a hand-painted, antique, wooden sledgehammer with an inscription artfully encrypted along its long, time-worn handle: "Viking Attitude Adjuster," it said.

Three areas were set up for entertainment. A small awning-covered wooden stage was set among the trees in a section of the park called "the grove"; a basketball court that stood in a small field between the park's playground and swimming pool served as the "main stage"; and the Vasa Cultural Center building not only handled those Swedish pancakes, but also served as the "music hall" to host various singers, musicians, and dancers.

The entertainment included the Scandinavian Accordion Club, Icelandic singers Sigridur Jonsdottir and Nina-Margret Grimsdottir, the Boston Scandinavian Ensemble (violin, recorder, guitar, and accordion), and at least three different Scandinavian folk-dancing groups. Two guys calling themselves "The Swede and the Norwegian" provided nonstop dancing music for everyone from 5:00 to 9:00 P.M.

Perhaps the best moments at a festival like this come from the small, seemingly inconsequential interactions. I loitered at the German Farms booth, for example, and learned quite a bit about the Celtic symbols. At the Hardanger fiddle and violin workshop, two professional string-playing women known as "The Daughters of Scandinavia" tutored a solitary student, a young lady of about twelve years, who was having the devil's time playing a certain sequence. One of the women calmly explained the passage to her several times, to no avail. Finally, she played it, and the child picked it up immediately. "Well, it's folk music," said the older musician, "it doesn't always sound like it looks."

We'd all gone our separate ways by then. When we all re-assembled to leave, I suddenly remembered those pancakes. I looked back.

"I didn't get any Swedish pancakes," I moaned. The line was longer than ever.

"I did," Leena said, grinning like a Cheshire cat.

"Should I get on line?"

"Oh no. It takes a long time," Leena replied. "They can only make them so fast."

"Were they good?"

She just smiled contentedly. My stomach growled. The mother in Leena took over. "Don't worry. I'll make you some sometime."

"Or, next year, I'll just get on that line first thing," I said, looking back wistfully as we exited.

Specifically: The Scandinavian Fest is in session all day Sunday on Labor Day weekend at Vasa Park in Budd Lake. The Fest is easily accessible from US 46; just turn onto Wolfe Road when you get to the west end of the lake and follow the signs. For schedule information and advance ticket forms (you save $2), call 610-868-7525 or 908-542-8150.

There is no lodging in Budd Lake, but the Festival brochure lists a number of nearby motels and bed and breakfasts.

32 Hoboken

Some call Hoboken "the square-mile city." From First to 13th Streets covers almost exactly a square mile. Some think of it as "the train place." North Jersey's commuter railroads end (or begin) here. Others think of Hoboken as the birthplace of Frank Sinatra and professional baseball. Still others, some 33,000 of them, think of Hoboken as home. But I think of Hoboken as the phoenix of New Jersey: the small city that has risen from semi-squalor and neglect to become a vital, vibrant, and stimulating town.

Hoboken is happening.

Let's start with that train station. Thousands of commuters pass through it daily. But for one day in October, the Hoboken train station becomes a railroad shrine. The Hoboken Train Festival revels in the magic of railroading. The main waiting room is transformed into a gigantic model train center. On the real tracks, antique engines and cars are driven in for display. Track repair equipment is demonstrated, the "Great Train Robbery" reenacted, and railroad memorabilia of all kinds is brought out of mothballs. The train festival even celebrates bus and ferry transportation by offering special rides.

But Hoboken lives beyond the train station. It was the artists who brought vitality back to this dormant city. Priced out of New York City's Greenwich Village and SoHo sections, they began drifting across the river. Why not? Hoboken townhouses rivaled Manhattan's. There were unused industrial spaces that could be transformed just as perfectly into lofts and studios as those in Brooklyn. Plus, not only did Hoboken offer easier Manhattan access, the cost of living and taxes were far lower. So the artists came. The financial workers, the young yuppie couples, and the recent college grads followed. They bought and renovated the houses and rejuvenated the town. Today the tales of the young couples who bought their home for $25,000 and could now sell it for upwards of $1 million are common. For visitors, this rejuvenation brings other benefits. Consider Washington Street, the town's main drag. The street bustles with an eclectic collection of restaurants, shops, bars, and clubs. Maxwell's, at 1039 Washington Street, is the best-known of the music spots. Often frequented by major rock bands and performers on their way to and from gigs in the Big Apple or Giants Stadium, this small bar has developed a large reputation as *the* place for great rock. But it's just one of many hot spots—there were at least a dozen clubs at my last count—for music and libations along Washington Street.

Washington Street shopping ranges from art and artifacts to scuba gear, snowboards, and skateboards. A stop at Cheap Maggie's should be on any itinerary; the little shop proffers an eclectic collection of Hoboken memorabilia, T-shirts, and name-brand clothing seconds. At Schnackenberg's Confectionery, a true old-time soda fountain, you can sip a "phosphate" the way mom and dad did when they dated.

If you prefer your dining and entertainment with a view, Hudson Street's restaurants whet the appetite with classic Manhattan vistas.

As might be expected in a town revitalized by artists, the arts thrive here. The Renegade Theater Company and the Waterfront Ensemble make Hoboken their home. Just north, in Union City, the Park Theater presents performances of all kinds in a magnificent Broadway-style, 1,400-seat theater built in the 1920s. The Park Theater has presented its annual "Easter Passion Play" for eighty years. Using a mixed cast of professionals and parish members, the spectacle has gained a reputation for excellence that brings audience members from far and wide, including from Manhattan, theater capital of America.

Hoboken's newest annual event is its September Washington

Street Art and Music Festival, in which the main thoroughfare is transformed into a street fair. The express purpose of the fair is to show off local talent – performers, musicians, and visual artists – and display the town's family spirit.

One of Hoboken's longest-standing annual events may also be one of its best-kept secrets. Let's call it "The Night Before Macy's" celebration. It goes like this. At Hoboken's northern end, just south of the entrance to the Lincoln Tunnel, stands a nondescript warehouse. Inside this warehouse are built and stored all the great floats for the annual New York City Macy's Thanksgiving Day Parade, among the country's two or three best-known parades. During the evening preceding the parade, the warehouse is open to the public and, if you get there early (just around dinner time) you can often catch the artists at work, finishing up with last-minute adjustments. If they're not too frazzled, you can catch their ear and get them talking about their work.

Shortly after that, about 8:30 P.M., the floats that will dazzle the nation the next day on TV emerge onto Willow Street. In a three-block-long procession, this "parade preview" travels into the Lincoln Tunnel and on into Manhattan. The "Night Before Macy's" is an informal event. It was described to me by one local as, "totally disorganized, but we want it that way." Which just goes to show you that even though Hoboken is gentrified, it hasn't lost its sense of fun.

Specifically: Hoboken can be reached by New Jersey Transit commuter trains or buses or by car from the Lincoln and Holland Tunnel access roads. Be aware that on Thursday, Friday, and Saturday nights, on-street parking can be very scarce; public parking lots are located on the south end of town and along Frank Sinatra Drive. A weekly newspaper, the *Hudson Current* (201-798-7800), lists events and entertainment.

33 September at the Shore
Stone Harbor and Tuckerton

The Wings 'n Water Festival

A series of large posters adorns the back wall of the Wetlands Institute's meeting room. They document the "Save the Terrapin Project." Each year female adult turtles seek high ground to lay their eggs, but along the way, many of these moms are killed by automobiles. Wetlands Institute volunteers collect the unhatched eggs, incubate them, and nurse the newborn turtles until they're large enough to venture off on their own. Partial funding for this noble project is generated by turtle-shaped cookies baked and sold by Avalon-Stone School kindergarten students, who also earn the right to help release the young turtles into the wild. Nearly 900 infant terrapins were given life in this manner last year, but more importantly, an attitude was instilled in young humans. It's that attitude that best describes the Wetlands Institute.

The Wetlands Institute sits on 6,000 salt marsh acres just west of Stone Harbor. The Institute works to further research and educate the public about the tidal wetlands and its inhabitants. For one glorious weekend in September, the Institute erupts into a beehive of activity that spills into Stone Harbor, Avalon, and Middle Township. They call it the Wings 'n Water Festival.

The Festival starts with an auction and VIP cocktail party on Friday evening; items for sale have included vacations, Broadway show tickets, and works of art. Come Saturday morning, the joint really starts rocking, with something for just about anyone. Naturalists conduct dune walks in Avalon. Live folk music plays throughout the weekend. The North American Shorebird Carving Championships are judged at Avalon Community Hall. Care for a cruise? The good ship *Miss Avalon* sets off for a series of Back Bay Cruises. Other options include "marsh bingo" for the kids, duck painting, air-sea rescue demonstrations by the U.S. Coast Guard, salt marsh safaris, and, my favorite, the annual Clam Chowder Cook-Off Contest. (You can go to New England, but you won't find better clam chowder, I promise.)

Of course, most visitors want more to eat than just clam chowder, and delicious food is available in great quantity. Especially worthy of note: the Stone Harbor Lutheran Church's Saturday brunch; "Something Fishy" at the Stone Harbor Fire House; and the Middle Township Chamber of Commerce flounder dinner at the Methodist Church, also on Saturday.

Between bites, you'll find ample opportunity to explore the marshlands and oceanfront and to learn how vital these delicate and changeable environments are. You'll also be helping an important institution to do its indispensable work.

The Decoy and Gunning Show

Tuckerton, sited just south of Long Beach Island on State 9, was settled in 1698 and known as Clamtown. The name changed in 1789 to honor Ebenezer Tucker, who had been Collector at Clamtown, the country's third official Port of Entry (behind New York and Philadelphia). But clamming remained the town's reason for being for many years. Some 60,000 clams were shipped daily from Tuckerton at the turn of this century. Active trade in oystering, fishing, hunting, boat building, and decoy making were carried out here, as well.

The Barnegat Bay Decoy and Baymen's Museum pays tribute to tiny Tuckerton's rich history with rotating and permanent displays, research, and continued restoration of the old seaport along the banks of Tuckerton Creek. Each year it salutes the traditions of Barnegat Bay, life in the Pinelands, and the skills of the region's outdoors and boat enthusiasts with its Old Time Barnegat Bay Decoy and Gunning Show.

The show sets up in three locations: indoor exhibits and

presentations are mounted at Pinelands Middle School and Pinelands High School, and tent exhibitions, local food concessions (featuring more remarkable clam chowder), and demonstrations take place along the tree-lined shores of Lake Pohatcong. How popular is the Decoy and Gunning Show? In the words of my friend Bob – hunter, fisherman, and Long Beach Island homeowner – "Basically, I think all of Ocean County turns out."

The show educates and entertains with displays by dozens of woodcarvers, naturalist artists, and jewelry makers; with the unique sounds of Pinelands musicians; and with talks and presentations on everything from Lyme disease and "Ghosts of the Pines" to hypothermia and "backyard birds in winter." But to me, it's the contests that make this event special.

It starts with a preliminary round of skeet shooting from a singular boat called a "sneakbox." Then the puppies show their stuff in the puppy retrieving contest. Kids get into the act at the kids' duck- and goose-calling seminar, and the boatmakers have their moment at the gunning boats accessories contest and the working shorebird rigs demo. The 1994 show program listed thirty-four of these events lasting most of the weekend.

Come Saturday evening, everyone sashays over to the high school cafeteria for the big spaghetti dinner, proceeds of which benefit the school's student organizations. After dinner, bidding opens at the "Annual Decoy and Related Items Auction" in the school auditorium. The auction, which, according to the show's official program, features "decoys by many old-time Barnegat Bay carvers," benefits the Baymen's Museum Building Fund.

The Baymen's Museum is at the center of it all. At present, the museum is small, but expansion plans have been formulated. The museum currently contains artifacts and thousands of photographs chronicling the Barnegat Bay area's culture. It is there that you'll discover everything there is to know about sneakboxes: twelve-foot-long, shallow-drafting wooden boats designed specifically to handle the rough Barnegat Bay winters. The original one, built in 1836, is displayed. You'll also find Barnegat Bay–style wildfowl decoys and fishery items (such as eeling baskets and oyster tongs), and a rotating display of local prize-winning carvers.

Together, these festivals add up to fascinating fun.

Specifically: The Wetlands Institute (609-368-1211) is located on Stone Harbor Boulevard in Stone Harbor; take the Garden State Parkway to Exit 10, then drive four miles east; the Institute is on the right. The Wet 'n Wild Festival takes place in mid-September and does have an admission fee.

The Barnegat Bay Decoy and Baymen's Museum (609-296-8868) is located at 137 West Main Street (US 9) in Tuckerton. Admission to the festival is free, and it takes place toward the end of September.

34 Fall Foliage

A Vermont friend calls them "leaf peepers," the tourists who drive past her house at five miles per hour gawking at the fall colors. But you needn't journey to New England to see spectacular foliage. In the mountains and rural parts of the New Jersey the show ranks with the best in the east. Indeed, when the leaf display is at its most radiant, a drive on almost any nonurban street or highway will dazzle your eye; even my daily carpool to gymnastics along well-developed I-80 becomes an eye-dazzler in mid- to late October.

New Jersey's north-to-south length means that peak foliage season can be stretched for two to three weeks. If your schedule causes you to miss the main event up north, you can still take it in down south.

It's impossible, of course, to list all the great places to go leaf peeping, but here are a few that stand out.

High Point State Park. Can there be a better place to witness the colorful splendor than the state's highest point? A climb up the park's 220-foot obelisk-style tower seems the obvious thing to do, but the small, barren, concrete chamber at the zenith contains only tiny, barred windows. The best views are found at the monument's base, sitting or standing on its stone retaining wall. The panorama expands for miles in all directions, and it takes in lakes, rivers, and the hills of Pennsylvania and southern New York. The visual reward is worth the trip. Follow State 23 almost as far north as it goes. High Point offers plenty of picnicking sites and hiking trails, too.

Palisades Interstate Park. Once upon a time the Palisades along the Hudson River supplied New York City and Hoboken with tons of brownstone from which the famous brownstone townhouses were constructed. Palisades Interstate Park was

130

created to preserve what remained unspoiled of the river's spectacular clifflands, and today the park provides a marvelously mixed visual delight.

The Palisades' hiking trails follow the river's shoreline from Fort Lee, just south of the George Washington Bridge, northbound to Hastings-on-Hudson in New York. Side trails along the way ascend and descend the bluffs.

Start under the G.W. Bridge. If you retain any of the typical three-year-old's construction wonder, walking under the bridge will provide a kind of erector-set visual excitement. Heading north, the riverside route reveals splendid and powerful views of the cliffs, made honey-sweet and tea-time warm by the Candyland colors. When you round the bend and the Tappan Zee Bridge (which spans the Hudson at its widest point) comes into view, the combination of man-made and natural spectacle stops you in your tracks. Although the Tappan Zee is often a nightmare to drive, its curved roadway exudes a majestic grace that somehow contrasts to and blends strikingly with the land and riverscape.

Turn back south now, and you'll be rewarded by another unique combination of man-made and natural spectacle – the Manhattan skyline across the water, the wide river, and the high cliffs that loom over your right shoulder. Talk about power.

The Delaware Water Gap. The Gap is spectacular at any time of the year, but add abundant splashes of color and the effect is dizzying. Hike the hills, float on the river, or just sit and stare for incredible views. Take the riverside drive along Old Mine Road, or simply ogle the Gap from the back porch of the Kittatinny Visitors Center, just off I-80.

The Navasink River By Boat. This is yet another of those "forgotten" or "unseen" bits of Jerseyana that pass unnoticed when you zip along only the state's highways, in this case the Garden

State Parkway. Captain Rich Moore's vessel, *The Teal*, leaves from Highlands and explores the Navasink River from its mouth, at Sandy Hook Bay inland, to the Red Bank area. During fall, the foliage dances along the river's high banks, revealing riverviews and landscapes that are as startling for their obscurity (how did I not know this was here?) as for their beauty. For river cruise information, call 908-957-9714.

Jenny Jump State Forest. One of New Jersey's smaller state reserves, Jenny Jump offers easy-to-get-to views from its main drive, Vista East Road, and fine visual rewards for hikers along the Summit Trail. Jenny Jump is just outside the town of Hope and is accessible from County 519.

The Great Swamp/Lord Stirling Park. Here's an excellent opportunity to see fall foliage wetlands style. The park, located not far from I-287 in Basking Ridge, contains about 8.5 miles of wide, flat trails, including a special interpretive nature trail for hikers who are blind or in wheelchairs. This is true swamp and wetlands, so many of the trails are actually raised boardwalks that make the going as easy as it is intriguing; the hickory, beech, and oak trees blend with the native grasses to put on one of the state's more complex color shows. The park's interpretive center sells trail maps.

Wharton State Forest. Start with a visit to the historical re-creation at Batsto Village (see Chapter 21), and pay a visit to the little Nature Center there. The naturalist on duty is delighted to share insights into the natural treasures of the area. Nearby, you'll find the Batsto Natural Area nature trail. The center prints a guide to the trail and sometimes offers guided hikes.

When you're ready for more prolonged exploration, join the Batona Trail (see Chapter 8), a fifty-mile wilderness path that traverses the Pine Barrens and roams through Wharton, Lebanon, and Bass River State Forests. Most of it is relatively easy walking.

Washington's Crossing State Park. Although Washington crossed the Delaware in the dead of winter, and his voyage is re-created each Christmas (see Chapter 49), dedicated leaf peepers will enjoy this riverside site, off State 29 north of Trenton, during late October. Another option in the area is to visit nearby Lambertville and walk or bike the path that parallels the Delaware River and Raritan Canal.

35 Victorian Week and Whale Watching
Cape May

Victorian Week

I dropped onto the bed in my room at the Virginia Hotel, too tired to take off my shoes, but craving a massage for my aching feet. Exploring Cape May – trying to see every last bit of Victoriana, to examine all the gingerbread latticework, and to admire each exquisite restoration – I'd walked myself into a state of exhaustion.

The name Cape May and the term Victorian have become synonymous. More than 600 authentic Victorian buildings stand within the town, and many modern homes have been built in the Victorian style. There is, indeed, more Victoriana than the eye can absorb, and the plethora of marvelous structures that line the quaint, narrow back streets and broad ocean-front boulevard present a walker's paradise. Armed with a good pair of shoes and a sunny day, a visitor can walk here for hours, marveling at the grand scale of the homes with their romantic pastel colors, or studying the dazzling architectural details. Whenever you think you've studied them all, another pops into view.

Cape May bills itself as "America's Oldest Seashore Resort." It traces its vacationing tradition to a June 1766 advertisement placed in the *Pennsylvania Gazette* by Robert Parsons, a local farmer, extolling the wonders of Cape May's ocean bathing and offering to accept paying guests at his large farmhouse. It was a crude and rudimentary beginning, and it didn't take immediately, but after the War of 1812, the Cape began to come into its own.

In mid-century, the advent of train travel helped Cape May grow. Still, it was, as the realtors say, location, location, location that engendered the town's visitor-attracting advantage. Sited at the very southern tip of New Jersey, folks were readily drawn from Philadelphia, Baltimore, and, most importantly, from Washington, DC. Indeed, Cape May and the nation's capital sit at the same latitude, and fashionable Washingtonians could readily get here by boat. Plus, the Cape had what was called the "twenty-degree advantage." Being set on a peninsula, with the benefit of ocean and bay cross-breezes (a sort of natural cross-ventilation) keeps summertime temperatures considerably cooler than those on the mainland.

The little city gets its current character not from its natural blessings, but from calamity. An 1878 fire destroyed almost everything in the thirty-acre heart of town. Landowners took the opportunity to rebuild in the fashionable style, but did so with superior quality and a close attention to detail. The result is the rich cache of Victorian houses we so admire today.

During early October, the town celebrates its wealth of Victoriana with its Victorian Week. The celebration includes events of all kinds, but, fittingly, walking tours are among the most abundant of the special offerings. Some of the tour possibilities include: the Stained Glass Tour, an evening affair in which participants are asked to bring a flashlight; the Historic District Walk, with guides providing detailed descriptions of Victorian lifestyles; an Ocean Walk along the beachfront with special attention to flora and fauna; a Champagne Brunch Walk that culminates with mimosas and a Southern-style breakfast; the Cape May Innteriors walk, focusing on bed-and-breakfast homes; and Victorian Homes and Gardens, which looks at private gardens not normally open to the public.

Victorian Week isn't all walking. You can tour the town by trolley and the surrounding waters by boat, or you can attend any number of special programs that include a crafts show, an antique dealers' gathering, a Victorian sing-along, a ragtime musical gala, a Victorian fashion show, a number of lecture/ demonstrations, and a Victorian mystery dinner, among others.

One tour that is offered year-round and should not be missed is the guided exploration of the Emlen Physick House. Designed by architect Frank Furness (best known for his work on Philadelphia's Academy of Fine Arts), the eighteen-room mansion was built in the 1870s, and for years it stood as Cape May's architectural centerpiece. Time and neglect eventually brought it to such disrepair that by 1970, its fame stemmed not from its lineage but from its reputation for being haunted. Just in time, however, the Mid-Atlantic Center for the Arts (MAC) was formed and the home was saved.

The Emlen Physick House tour is led by remarkably well-informed volunteers who mix a vibrant and lively collection of historical fact, fiction, and insight with personal perspective, experience, and anecdotes—all delivered in a personable manner that holds the entire group's attention without sway. Even the children who toured with us remained fascinated throughout.

Cape May offers more than Victoriana, of course, and once I'd gotten my feet back into working order, I set out to seek the great whales.

Whale Watching

The fog rolled in. The boat rolled out. Quietly it slipped under Cape May Island Bridge, traveling through water droplets suspended in midair and over those that made up the ocean. I conjured visions of Gregory Peck in the Hollywood version of Melville's epic *Moby Dick*.

A true landlubber, I prepped for the journey quite differently from the way Ahab might have, with a motion sickness pill for breakfast and a vow to avoid the ship's snack bar, except perhaps to purchase popcorn. Popcorn, it turns out, is favored by gulls. All we need do, Captain Ron informed us over the loudspeaker, was stand at the side rail with a morsel held lightly between thumb and forefinger. The birds would eat right from our hands.

Chugging along, we received instructions to scan the horizon, just where the sky meets the water (although the fog rendered the sky and sea indistinguishable from each other). Look, we were told, for grand plumes of water—whales spouting. Search, we were admonished, for enormous black blobs flopping against the blue-gray background—whales breaching. Scan constantly, we were beseeched, for whales are not particularly trackable by radar or sonar. For the longest time, no luck. Then I saw it! A big, black . . . Or did I? Guess not. Just a wave catching a little light at just the wrong angle. But wait! A shout from the kids on the bow! Oops. A commercial fishing ship approaching in the mist.

Three hours passed. Our chances of seeing whales grew as dim as the visibility. Captain Ron and his assistant, a naturalist named Kelly, did their best to keep us from giving up, educating us nonstop over the loudspeaker about whales and sea birds. We searched to the very end. To quote Melville's narrator Ishmael, "Not till her skysail-poles sail in among the spires of the port, does she altogether relinquish the hope of capturing one whale more." Or, in our case, seeing one whale at all. Alas, it was to no avail. In seeking the whale we got skunked. But we received coupons to try again another day at half-price, and, even without whales, we had a good time.

Specifically: The Cape May Chamber of Commerce, PO Box 556, Cape May, NJ 08204 (609-884-5508) sponsors special events year-round and publishes an avalanche of literature offering general and events information and lodging help. Overnight accommodations run the gamut from large hotels to small motels, bed and breakfasts, and campgrounds. I count the

Virginia Hotel (800-732-4236 or 609-884-5700) among the best small hotels I've ever experienced.

House tours of the Emlen Physick Estate and town trolley tours are conducted by the Mid-Atlantic Center for the Arts (609-884-5404); call for schedules.

Whale Watching is best done in the early spring or fall. A number of shore locations offer the opportunity. The New Jersey Division of Travel and Tourism's Outdoor Guide contains a list of companies; call 1-800-537-7397 to obtain a copy. For information on Cape May whale watching, call 609-898-0280.

36 A Classic College Town
Princeton

It was a brilliantly sunny November. We strolled across the Princeton University campus, arching our necks to admire the Gothic architecture. At a place where several walkways crossed, we passed a professorial-looking gentleman, perhaps in his early sixties, dressed in a Harris tweed coat and tie. He smiled amiably to himself. Had he been carrying books or a briefcase, we could have assumed he was on his way to or from an important academic lecture. But this was Saturday, and under his arm he held a pair of stadium seat cushions, brightly decorated in Princeton Tigers' black and orange. Our professor had apparently come from today's game at Palmer Stadium. He was smiling, no doubt, over the final score: Princeton 20, Dartmouth 13.

A fall football weekend visit to Princeton, a pretty, prestigious town along the Delaware and Raritan Canal, is the stuff of classic Hollywood imagery. Ivy League football is played with the perfect combination of prowess and perspective; the athletes are good, but there are no athletic scholarships and a true spirit of amateur athletics prevails. The kids play hard and for the love of the game. The pep and pageantry stem from true school spirit, not the hope of filling the school coffers by winning a place in a major bowl game or so-called national championship. Kick-off time is 1:00 P.M., but if you arrive early and join the alumni and other faithful for a tailgate picnic in the parking lot, you'll get the full flavor of the day.

After the game, tour the campus. Stop first at either the University Bookstore or Stanhope Hall and pick up a guidebook. It will not only fill you in on all the sculpture, art, and architecture you'll see, but it'll prove indispensable when trying to locate any specific building. Believe me, we tried getting around without one and learned what it meant to be like lost sheep. Formal, "Orange Key" tours are conducted by gregarious and enthusiastic university students. The kids give an insider's insight into the history and what's current at the university.

We exchanged "hellos" with the cheerful professor, and entered Nassau Hall, the oldest building on campus. The entry hall, a stark, marble-walled war memorial, somberly displayed engraved listings of Princetonians who had given their lives in wars dating back to the Revolution. Sobered, we encountered a student who entered as we exited. His long hair flowing out from under a 1910 straw, skimmer hat, he sported a striped blazer and carried an all-in-one, pep band bass-drum-and-noisemaker set strapped to his chest. An orange-and-black-striped tiger tail flopped from his hat's rear brim. The building and the student created a vivid picture: heritage, modernity, and tradition, all rolled into one.

We walked to the university chapel. Built in the 1920s, it is a classic piece of Gothic Revival architecture. A descriptive pamphlet is available as you enter the building. It details such particulars as the figure of James Madison (Class of 1771) depicted in one of the tall stained-glass windows. Madison championed Article I of the Bill of Rights, making religious freedom a basic tenet, making his a particularly appropriate image for this church. It notes, as well, that the oaken pews were constructed from wood originally intended for use as gun carriages during the Civil War.

Next door, in the Firestone Library's Rare Books section, the impressive collection is complemented by a rotating exhibit that explores the historical uses of books. We saw a display on Islamic culture and Quar'an (Koran), featuring handwritten books dating to very ancient times. Upstairs and to the rear is hidden the Leonard L. Millberg Gallery; you may have to ask to find it, but it's worth it. We discovered a fascinating exhibit of children's book illustrations there.

Blair Hall's Gothic arch frames Lockhart Hall at Princeton

The Art Museum at McCormick Hall houses an eyeball-wrenching collection of classic paintings. The great impressionists, great portrait artists, and classic landscapers adorn nearly every square inch of wall space; impressive, but overwhelming.

Beyond the campus, Princeton offers a number of historical sites. These include two houses that once were home to Woodrow Wilson, one that was the childhood residence of singer-actor Paul Robeson, and another where Albert Einstein lived. At the corner of Nassau Street and Washington Road, you'll find the Historical Society, housed in a classic Georgian home. The society offers a wealth of information and guided Sunday afternoon historical tours.

Downtown Princeton, along Nassau Street and at Palmer Square, offers shopping that leans to well-known names in upscale clothes, jewelry, and so on, plus a sprinkling of art galleries, bookstores, and music shops. Of course, you can purchase almost any kind of Princeton University paraphernalia. A swing down Witherspoon Street takes you to some shops with a bit less polish and some interesting bargains.

The performing arts, too, flourish in Princeton. The McCarter Theater can be counted among the finer regional theaters in the country, and professional and collegiate music, theater, and dance performances are plentiful. We wandered, lost, for half an hour in search of an auditorium that nobody seemed to have heard of (yes, we should have bought that campus guide first). When we finally located the place, we enjoyed a very pleasant free concert of works by Bartok, Ives, Hayden, and Copland performed by the Princeton University Chamber Orchestra, an ensemble composed largely of freshmen and sophomores. After each piece, the performers' friends and roommates literally cheered for their musician schoolmates, not unlike many of them had no doubt done for their athlete schoolmates that very afternoon at the stadium. But in the concert hall, few wore black and orange, and nobody carried a tiger's tail.

Specifically: Princeton is located just off US 1, which can be accessed from the Garden State Parkway, the New Jersey Turnpike, or I-95/295. The town can be reached by train from New York City's Penn Station; call 1-800-772-2222 for schedule and fare information.

General information and the "Princeton Visitor's Guide" are available by calling 609-520-1776, 609-921-7676, or 609-683-1760.

U.S. 1 Newspaper publishes a useful seasonal guide to the Princeton area, which can be obtained at area hotels, the news kiosk in Palmer Square, or by calling 609-452-0038.

For football ticket information, call 609-258-3538. For campus walking-tour information, call 609-258-3603; or, for historical walking-tour information, call 609-921-6748.

37 Outlet Shopping
Secaucus and Flemington

Secaucus

Secaucus was once the butt of many pejorative New Jersey jokes. No wonder. The town stood at the edge of an expansive swamp and was the site of several large pig stockyards and slaughterhouses. Between the mosquitoes and the smell, Secaucus never had a chance.

That changed when warehouses began popping up in the town. A number of big-name Manhattan fashion and garment houses took to storing their goods in New Jersey. These fashion trendsetters soon discovered that they could unload their unsold or slightly blemished goods right from their warehouses. It seemed that the same adventurous spirit that will drive some people to compulsively scour for bargains among the lofts of Manhattan would also drive them to explore the industrial backroads of New Jersey. Secaucus, after all, lies only a few minutes' drive from the Lincoln Tunnel. And more importantly *there is no sales tax on clothing in New Jersey!*

Secaucus discount shopping remains hidden among the warehouses and trucking depots. Therefore, to thrive or even survive in Secaucus, you must: (1) have a car and (2) stop at the first available shopping site and grab the area guides – "Secaucus Guide Book" or "Secaucus Outlet Centre." (Take both; not every shop is listed in each.) Without these maps, you may be doomed to wander aimlessly for hours.

We started at a place called Outlets at the Cove on Meadowlands Parkway. Careful – it's easily missed. We picked up the magazines here, and we found two stores offering excellent bargains on the Bugle Boy and Van Heusen brands. I bought my extra-large-sized, ultra-picky teenaged son a collared Bugle Boy polo shirt for five dollars, and bought myself a Van Heusen broadcloth dress shirt for twelve. We were both happy.

A few blocks south, on the left, another super find awaits discovery – A Real New York Bargain. Ten dollars is the highest price you'll pay for almost anything among the store's hodge-podge collection of clothing that includes everything from pure silk blouses and Izod shirts to real junk. It takes a sharp shopper's eye to get the most from "the ten dollar store" (plus timing, since the stock can turn over daily), but the bargains make it very worthwhile. You say that a ten-dollar outlet isn't inexpensive enough? Well, A Real New York Bargain has its own outlet's outlet several doors down, in which most items sell for five bucks.

If name brands are more your style, there's hardly one you can't find somewhere in the Secaucus labyrinth. Several vendors offer more than one location. Among the visitors' musts: London Fog, Gucci, Sango, Suzell/Stephanie, and the European Outlet for clothes; Harvey Electronics for high-tech and hi-fi; Marty's Shoes; Enterprise Golf; and the Door Store for furniture. Another wonderful secret is the Playground Warehouse, which is almost impossible to find without getting lost at least twice. In a warehouse with ceilings at least twenty-five-feet high, a wonderful array of backyard and institutional swingsets and large plastic toys are displayed. Best of all, the floors are covered in rubberized outdoor play matting, so you can bring your kids and let them explore and test the toys to their heart's content.

Just one caution about Secaucus shopping: expect to get lost. It helps to turn the shopping guide map upside down as you navigate. I'm not sure why.

Flemington

While Secaucus sits right next door to Manhattan, Flemington can be said to be located in the middle of nowhere. What could make Flemington a discount shopping center?

I don't know. But the Flemington Cut Glass Company

anticipated the trend. They've been selling factory seconds here since 1920.

I drove into town on a day heavy with rain, accompanied by my two expert shopping consultants—my then thirteen-year-old daughter Laina and her pal, Megan. We approached from the north via State 31, a far more scenic and pleasant approach than that afforded by commercially cluttered US 202. By approaching from the road less traveled, our first impression of the village came from its downtown. Main Street in Flemington has character. It also has history. Many of the town's buildings are listed on the state and national historic registers, but perhaps the most famous is the imposing Greek Revival County Courthouse on Main Street, site of the 1935 Lindbergh kidnapping trial. The trial drew national attention, and its outcome—a guilty verdict for, and the execution of, immigrant carpenter Bruno Hauptmann—remains controversial to this day. The courthouse lobby displays fascinating Lindbergh memorabilia. Between court sessions, newspaper and radio reporters took refuge across the street in the Union Hotel, another charismatic building worthy of a visit. For overnight visitors, two of the state's more pleasant Victorian bed and breakfasts—the Cabbage Rose and the Jessica Hill Inn—grace the heart of town. Alas, I was not allowed to linger. My traveling companions were impatient to get to the meat of the matter. We followed the signs to Liberty Village.

Liberty Village, its management proudly declares, was "the first 'outlet village' of its kind." Exactly what kind of outlet village is it? Well, even a shopping curmudgeon like me will admit it's a very pleasant one. Done in neo-colonial architecture with rich, red brick walkways, there really is a village feeling. There are sixty stores here, ranging from Brooks Brothers to Royal Doulton to the nifty THE Housewares Store (I just love shops full of kitchen gadgets). The kids gravitated toward the Champion Hanes Activewear Outlet and the Bass Clothing

Outlet. Somehow, they weren't moved by the Brooks Brothers or Jones New York offerings. We peeked in on the required big names—Anne Klein, Harvé Benard, Donna Karan, and Calvin Klein, and stopped in at the Bucks Country Cafe for some scrumptious cookies.

When the rain made it too awkward to ramble outdoors, we scooted next door to the Feed Mill Plaza. It really was an old feed mill, although you have to approach it from the rear to fully appreciate that fact. Now, with a classy glass facade and entry-way, it has been converted into two upscale-looking floors of shops.

We finished our tour with a stop at Flemington's most famous store, Flemington Fur. We came only to see the famous shrine, not to shop it. Good thing. They'd just closed.

Altogether, Flemington offers 120 outlet stores. As in Secaucus, a magazine guide is published. Pick one up almost anywhere in town. You can break up your shopping spree with an hour-and-a-half scenic ride on the restored steam train of the Black River & Western Railroad. Or just go ahead and shop till you drop.

Specifically: Many of the outlets in both Secaucus and Flemington are closed in the evenings; those that do stay open most likely only do so on Thursdays.

To reach Secaucus from the east or west, take State 3 to the Meadowlands Parkway exit. From the north or south, take the New Jersey Turnpike or Garden State Parkway to State 3 east, and exit at Meadowlands Parkway.

To reach Flemington from the north, take I-80 west to I-287 south, and exit onto US 202 south; from the south, take I-95/295 exit onto State 31 north, and then take US 202 north. Daily bus service leaves from New York City's Port Authority Bus Station, call 1-800-962-9135 for bus information.

For general Flemington information, call the information center at 908-806-8165 between 9:00 A.M. and 5:00 P.M. Monday through Friday, or call the Flemington Business Association at 908-284-8118. A free trolley circulates throughout business hours.

38 Canoeing in the Pinelands
Jackson

Ed Mason drops the canoe into the murky water. Not ten feet above us and twenty feet away vehicles rush over a highway viaduct. But down here among the thick brambles and knotted trees, we're in another world.

We climb aboard, gently push off, pass under the highway, and begin to ease on down the stream. After a few bends in the river, we pass the last houses of a nearby development, and we enter the timeless wilderness of the northern Pinelands.

The north branch of the Toms River runs parallel to County 527 out of Jackson and eventually empties into Barnegat Bay at the town of Toms River. We're paddling a section that Ed describes as "winding and narrow, but safe enough." The current flows at a deceptive five knots. The river seems placid, but when we negotiate its many hairpin turns, we require quick reactions to keep the canoe from hanging up in the weeds, grounding on a rock, or getting snared by the dense thicket that overruns the riverbanks.

"Duck!" Ed calls. I look up, expecting to see a mallard flying overhead. Instead, I come within a hair's breadth of smacking my forehead on a tree trunk—the water is half-bridged by profuse low-clearance, overhanging tree trunks.

The Toms' shores are dense with river beech, holly, oak, and maple. Here and there you find stands of pine. You're never really far from development here, but the woods are deep enough to create the wilderness feeling. The lack of other on-river travelers reinforces that sense. "There's canoeing down in Wharton State Park, but on the weekends it's as busy as Disney World," Ed comments.

Among the animals to look for, Ed lists beaver, river otters, and ducks. Blue heron frequent the river in the spring, and owls are a common sight. "Some people claim that they've been attacked by the owls," Ed tells me. "But actually, the owl needs to dive to pick up enough air speed to fly off. It's really trying to get out of the way."

Ed Mason, at sixty-six years of age, has been canoeing these parts for nearly six decades. A retired school teacher, he now devotes all his working hours to his canoe rental business, Pinelands Canoe. He does no guiding; indeed, Ed claims nobody runs guided canoe trips down here in the Pines. "The insurance costs too damned much," he mutters. For a reasonable fee, Ed will rent you a canoe, take you to the drop-off point, point you in the right direction, and pick you up at a designated pick-up point. "On this section of the Toms, you're not likely to get lost," he says. Farther south in the Pinelands, however, Ed cautions, the rivers and streams meander, fork, and cross, and you can become dangerously lost.

Ed's trips run from two hours to two days. If you want to camp overnight, he directs you to Riverwood Park in Dover Township. You need a permit to camp in Riverwood (and Ed will help you get one), but you can pitch your tent for free. As we approach a wide left-turning bend in the river, he decides to show me the campsites. We beach, disembark, and follow a well-worn path that first parallels the river, then turns sharply into the woods, and finally opens into a small clearing with two or three wilderness-style campsites. "This is where you'd spend the night," Ed announces. It would make a very pleasant place to camp, if camping is your cup of tea.

Back on the river, Ed talks about growing up in Trenton and paddling with his older brother from near here to the ocean when he was about ten years old. "My father was a builder," he says, "and he did a lot of work in Seaside Park. When we got to the mouth of the Toms, we had to paddle across Barnegat Bay. We made it, too."

We would encounter no such challenge on this trip. Too

soon we reach our take-out point–another highway overpass. Says Ed, "We've got two day-trip routes. Short and long. For the short one, you get out at the first overpass. For the long one, you get out at the second. We like to keep it simple." Altogether we'd paddled about five miles in just over two hours, a very pleasant trip, indeed, that could probably be handled by paddlers with only basic canoeing skills and experience. Next time, I think I'll go for the longer, two-overpass version.

Specifically: Pinelands Canoe (908-364-0389) offers canoe rentals from April through October; take State 70 to County 527 north, go four miles, and it's on the left.

The New Jersey Canoe Liveries Association lists member companies. Call Pinelands Canoe for a list.

The New Jersey Division of Travel and Tourism's Outdoor Guide lists a variety of canoe rental companies and canoe clubs; call 1-800-537-7397 for a copy.

39 All That Jazz (Plus Art, History, and Great Food), Newark

The sweet sounds emanating from the hotel ballroom are like the tip of an iceberg. What you hear is impressive and moving, but it's only a small part of the whole. The rest of the scene comprises a vast musical panorama that spans most jazz styles and includes many of its stars.

In just a handful of years, the Newark Jazz Festival has grown into one of the premier musical events in New Jersey. The quality and quantity of jazz artists who perform here could make up a significant portion of anyone's who's who list. Best of all, the festival provides an occasion to enjoy some of Newark's most fascinating places.

The festival includes some two dozen free concerts staged in all kinds of venues. There's the lunchtime "Jazz Break" series at office buildings sprinkled throughout downtown. Or the "Rush Hour Riffs" in Penn Station's main waiting room. Midday vibraphone offerings (called Jazz Vibes) take place at the Newark Public Library.

The ballroom session is held at the Robert Treat Hotel on Park Place. The Tri-State Ballroom is transformed into a cabaret-style club and functions as the site of a series of paid-admission concerts aptly called "Jazz Treats." Treats includes gigs by the likes of pianists Ramsey Lewis and Cyrus Chestnut, singers Diane Reeves and Jimmy Scott, and an all-female ensemble called the Kit McClure Big Band.

For those who prefer their jazz in a club setting, "Jersey Jazz Masters" takes place at a variety of the area's restaurant-clubs. Back at the Robert Treat Hotel, a Saturday afternoon "Invitational Improvisation Workshop," especially aimed at kids, gives everyone a chance to catch great musicians at their creative best.

The entire affair has been known to kick off with a symposium at the Newark Museum. That's a perfect example of what I mean when I say that, if you let it, the festival can take you to some of the city's great spots. Use the symposium as a good excuse to begin an exploration of the museum. The Newark Museum ranks among the premier institutions of its type in the country. Completely restored in 1989, the building houses sixty-six galleries and 60,000 square feet of exhibition space. The museum holds one of the most outstanding collections of American art in the world, ranging from colonial times to the present. The Asian collection features an internationally renowned assemblage of Tibetan works, and the classical collection contains some of the most remarkable pieces of ancient glasswork anywhere. Next door, the twenty-one-room Ballantine House is the only landmark, urban, Victorian mansion in the state open to the public. In addition to providing a unique study in and collection of Victoriana, Ballantine House also holds the museum's extensive decorative arts collection.

The Junior Museum conducts a series of weekend workshops for kids from six to sixteen. Activities range from constructing building models in the architecture workshop to drawing and painting sessions. The museum also offers a series of free special events for children. For adults, the museum offers subject-specific guided tours and operates a travel program.

Downtown Newark is also the site of Symphony Hall, home to the New Jersey Symphony orchestra and the setting for many other concerts. Considered an acoustical masterpiece, the hall is a wonderful place to listen to any kind of music.

If you're going to visit Newark, you'd better want to eat. Newark's Ironbound section has become famous for its selection of Spanish, Portuguese, and Italian restaurants. I'm not talking about the latest "hot spot," or the current "johnny-come-lately" darling of the nouveau cuisine set. I'm talking about places like the Spanish Tavern, which opened for business in 1932; the Iberia Tavern, in business for nearly seventy years; or even such "newcomers" as Roque & Robelo, which opened in the '60s, and the twenty-five-year-old Albin's Restaurant.

Like the "Jazz Treats," this sampling of Newark sites and eating spots represents just the tip of the iceberg. But it's more than enough to keep you going for most of the Jazz Festival's nine-day run. The whole affair reaches a unique and incredible finale with the annual "Key Club and Sparky J's Reunion." In the 1970s the Key Club and Sparky J's were Newark clubs that specialized in jazz played on the organ and by organ combos. The reunion brings together some half a dozen organists and a handful of drummers, trombonists, trumpeters, guitarists, and other musicians for one huge jam session. You won't find anything quite like it anywhere else. Except maybe at the next Newark Jazz Festival.

Specifically: The Newark Jazz Festival takes place in early November; call 201-643-3605 for schedule and ticket information.

The Newark Museum (201-596-6550) is located at 49 Washington Street; from the Garden State Parkway, take Exit 145 to I-280 east; from the New Jersey Turnpike, take Exit 15W to I-280 west; from I-280, take Exit 14-A, go right onto Martin Luther King Boulevard, then left at the third traffic light onto Central Avenue; the parking lot will be on your left in about a block.

For general Newark information, contact the Newark Meadowlands Convention and Visitors Bureau at 201-622-3010.

40 Cranberry Festival
Chatsworth

Let us now praise the great red berry – the cranberry, that is, a fruit that flourishes in the Pinelands. The berries grow in great sloughy bogs and are harvested by knocking them off their perches so they are freed to float in artificial lakes, then "raking" them "downstream" for collection in waist-deep water. In Chatsworth, home of an Ocean Spray juice factory, the cranberry harvest has long been an autumn tradition. At the turn of the century, pickers migrated to these fields on chartered trains out of Philadelphia to harvest the berries by hand. Today, the picking process is mechanized, and the harvest has become a wonderful excuse for this town of 200 to stage a festival.

The festival starts even before you get into town. For several miles to the east, County 532 is lined with makeshift roadside stands selling everything but the kitchen sink. Well, you just might find the kitchen sink, too. But don't tarry too long, for the show is just beginning.

In town, the festivities center around the landmark White Horse Inn, and everything turns berry, berry red: the clothes, candy, ornaments, hats, decorations, and even the ice cream cones. You might see the odd exception, like a clown sporting bright green or yellow hair, but rest assured, he'll boast a bright red nose. The mythical Jersey Devil, who is said to stalk the Pine Barrens, will be there, too, dressed in a red jacket.

Just when you think you've been seeing red long enough, you'll begin to discover that honoring the cranberry goes deeper than mere surface color. The fest presents an array of remarkably clever uses of the honored berry.

Cranberry crafts, anyone? There are bouquets, dolls, wreaths, and decorations of all kinds.

Even though we know that the cranberry is edible, the scope of foodstuffs into which the berry can be cooked will still surprise you; jelly, yes, and pies, of course. Cookies too, and jam, chutney, ices, tea and . . . oh yes, sauce. Do try the cranberry-topped funnel cakes. But the jury's still out on the cranberry pizza and the cranberry fudge. Me? I'll recommend any of the muffin offerings.

If you've any doubt about modern Chatsworthians' devotion to the cranberry, take a look at the biggest and smallest berries cultivated this year. You may need a magnifying glass to admire the smallest.

For the full background on this cranberry mania, stop in at the history tent. The festival is organized and mounted by something called the Chatsworth Club II. The club was founded to help restore the White Horse Inn, and it uses the proceeds from the festival to do that. But the original Chatsworth Club, established in 1900 or so, was something quite different. With a membership roll that included such names as Astor, DuPont, and Vanderbilt, the club was dedicated to hunting, fishing, hiking, and, no doubt, riding to the hunt. The inn is the sole building remaining of the many that club members erected.

Since you've traveled all this way, please don't bypass the bog tour. You must make advance reservations for the tour, but it's worth the commitment. It takes ten acres of water storage to farm one acre of cranberries. While flooding the bog is the preferred commercial juice- and sauce-harvesting method, the locals will tell you that the finest eating berries are dry-picked by hand. The difference was explained to me, but I'll not pretend I understood. Regardless, the wet-harvesting process is fascinating. The bog turns into a deep red lake from the millions of berries bobbing around in the water as the men, legs encased in long rubber boots, herd the fruit to capture and transport it to the factory. The color must be seen to be believed.

While the harvest may be the *pièce de résistance* of the festival, it's hardly the finale. You'll want to return to town to catch an impromptu pine cone music concert. You might think pine cone music is just bluegrass, but the "Pineys" put some unique instruments to work and create a singular sound.

Then there's the antique car parade, with the requisite award for the car wearing the best cranberry-colored coat of paint. The story-telling contest reveals much about local folkways, and the flea market behind the inn is a testament to the notion that one man's junk is another man's treasure.

Just one more stop before you leave. Buzby's general store. Built in 1865, Buzby's takes you time-traveling from those Civil War days to the early part of this century. Tables with red-checkered tablecloths, offerings of all kinds of goods, and that simple, pleasant old-time feeling of a time long past will make you appreciate that something personal and wonderful has been lost in our fast-paced, shopping-mall world.

Now, pick up a quart or two of cranberries and a copy of the festival's cookbook, and you're ready to take the Chatsworth tradition home. It's the berries.

Specifically: The Cranberry Fest runs over two weekends in early October. Call 609-859-9701 for event information.

To get there coming southbound on the Garden State Parkway, take Exit 67 and follow County 554 until it intersects with State 72 west; from the Parkway northbound, take Exit 63 directly onto State 72; follow State 72 about twelve miles, then go left onto County 532. Coming from the west, take Exit 4 from the New Jersey Turnpike, then follow State 73 south four miles; take a left onto State 70 east and travel about twenty miles before turning right onto State 72 east; in seven miles, turn right onto County 563 south.

41 Artists' Studio Tour
Liberty State Park and Ellis Island, Jersey City

Artists' Studio Tour

A recent survey offers a telling snapshot of Jersey City. In the homes of Jersey City school children, some ninety different languages are spoken. Talk about ethno-cultural diversity.

That survey illustrates Jersey City's traditional place as a haven for new arrivals from foreign lands. It started with the Dutch, who first settled here soon after Henry Hudson sailed into New York harbor and founded the state's first city of European origin. Later, in the boom immigration years of the late nineteenth and early twentieth centuries, Jersey City became the pivot point for tens of thousands who came from Europe. They got off the boat, were processed for immigration at Ellis Island, and then had two choices: take the ferry to New York City, or the ferry to Jersey City's grand Central Railroad Station. Of those who chose the latter, many boarded trains for points inland where relatives or friends awaited them. The others, however, made Jersey City their new home.

Goods as well as people traditionally came in and out of the country through Jersey City. First, ocean-going cargo traveled through on the Morris Canal. Later, the great railway lines transported the goods to and from Jersey City's docks. But time brought changes and decline. Container shipping caused the large docks to move to more modern Bayonne, nearby, and companies sought new sites where labor was cheaper.

Despite the decline, Jersey City today ranks as New Jersey's third-largest city, and it has begun a comeback. Like Hoboken before it, the Jersey City renaissance can be found in the growing arts community.

Artists – be they visual or performance artists – often represent the vanguard of a return to urban health. They are adept at converting old industrial habitats into magnificent living and work spaces. With its myriad antiquated factory buildings and warehouses, easy access to Manhattan, and low living costs, Jersey City makes sense for artists.

Each October, Jersey City celebrates its burgeoning art community with an Artists' Studio Tour. For one Sunday afternoon, professional artists throughout the community open their studios to the public to show their work, answer questions, share ideas, and, they hope, to sell their work. Performers and musicians participate, too, at more than forty public and private sites. A free shuttle bus transports visitors to key spots along the route.

The collection of studios at 111 First Street, an old P. Lorrilard Tobacco Company warehouse, typifies an artists' adapted industrial building. The labyrinthine halls of this five-story brick edifice house a sensational variety of media, styles, and artistic statements that represent a vibrant and eclectic mix. Not all of it necessarily meets your personal tastes, but the work provides wonderful surprises and constant stimulation.

A few blocks away at Grace Church, everything from photography to oil painting to sculpture with children's plastic building blocks might be on display, and performances include dance, storytelling, and poetry readings. In a small pocket park, a jazz ensemble plays. The Jersey City Museum features art with Jersey City themes, artists with Jersey City roots, and live music and performance. Even City Hall is crammed with visual displays. The tour route is compelling and fascinating – and plenty of wine and hors d'oeuvres are available along the way.

Liberty State Park and Ellis Island
Liberty State Park sits at the water's edge along Upper New York Bay. Comprising 1,114-acres, the park is an expansive urban greenspace and home to the Liberty Science Center (see Chapter 13). From here, the views from the waterside promenade take

Ellis Island and the ferry

in the Statue of Liberty, Ellis Island, and Manhattan–a superb cityscape–and access to the Statue of Liberty and Ellis Island is far easier from here than from across the Hudson. While a visit to the Statue of Liberty is probably a must-do for most visitors, for me the Ellis Island Immigration Museum is particularly special. The restoration of the main building and the presentation of the arriving immigrants' stories are beautifully rendered and extremely powerful. Many come to Ellis Island thinking that they'll spend an hour. Don't. Come early and be prepared to spend the better part of your day. Do rent a tape player and listen to the audio tour as you explore the three floors of exhibits. Do, without question, view the short but moving film that describes what it was like to arrive here from a far-away land and the agony of those who were detained or turned away.

In some ways, the newly restored building is a bit too sanitized. Yet it takes only a smidgeon of imagination, when you look at the entrance hall's large display of antique luggage or view the main hall's benches, to put yourself into these people's shoes.

Return to Liberty State Park and make two more stops. First, the Central Railroad Terminal. Often overlooked, it was the site that began the last stage of the immigrants' journey. Beautifully restored and now home to a variety of special events and festivals, the terminal completes the best picture of those times that we can muster today.

Lastly, venture south in the park, out past the park's offices toward the promenade, to view sculptor Natan Rapoport's statue "Liberation." Here, with Lady Liberty, the World Trade Center, and lower Manhattan as a backdrop, is depicted an American soldier carrying a concentration camp survivor to safety. Joined at the shoulder to represent them as one, as fellows of the human race, the sculpture offers tribute to what

161

we can only hope is the best and true meaning of military action – to protect and deliver the oppressed to freedom.

Specifically: The Artists' Studio Tour is sponsored by the *Jersey Journal* (201-217-2480) and takes place on a Sunday in early October.

Liberty State Park (201-915-3400) can be reached from the New Jersey Turnpike Exit 14-B; turn left and follow the signs. The park is open daily from 6:00 A.M. to 10:00 P.M.; its office is open from 6:00 A.M. to 6:00 P.M.

Liberty State Park hosts a number of festivals throughout the year, the most spectacular of which is the American Heritage Festival (201-915-1212), an enormous and gala celebration of American history that is staged in October.

Ellis Island (212-363-7620) and the Statue of Liberty (212-363-3200) are open daily from 9:00 A.M. to 5:00 P.M. Both are accessible from Liberty State Park by the Circle Line Ferry (201-435-9499).

The Central Railroad Terminal (201-915-3400) is open during daylight hours, and offers special exhibits during the summer.

Winter

42 Yes, You Can Ski Here

The older gentleman joined me on the chairlift, and we rode together toward the snowfields that awaited us 10,000 feet up in the Wyoming sky. We exchanged the usual skier-to-skier pleasantries – the weather, the wonderful snow conditions, and eventually, where we each lived. An Idaho Falls, Idaho, native, he did a startled double-take when I said, "New Jersey."

"Jersey, eh? No skiing there, I reckon."

"Oh sure there is," I answered, as I had to so many westerners so many times before. "I learned to ski in New Jersey."

It's not unusual to find denizens of the Rocky Mountain states, or even New England, who find it hard to believe there could be real alpine skiing in New Jersey. I can remember being equally surprised at the notion when plans for construction of the first large ski area were announced. Some entrepreneurial types cut ski runs and installed lifts in McAfee, a small town in Sussex County. They called their "resort" Great Gorge. Soon, Vernon Valley appeared next door. Several years later, when I was sixteen, two friends took me to Great Gorge, and I began a pastime that quickly developed into a passion.

With modern snowmaking and snow-grooming technology, skiing in New Jersey has become more than viable. It has become a strong recreational attraction. Although the state houses

165

but four ski areas (plus what I'd call a "town hill" outside of Lambertville), its major area, the now-merged Vernon Valley/ Great Gorge, can be called a true resort. With fifty-two trails and seventeen lifts, a full complement of condominiums, restaurants, and a health spa, it is likely to be among the busiest ski areas in the east on any given winter weekend. To obtain a mountain resort hotel ambience, visit Seasons Resort across the valley, just five minutes' drive from the lifts.

Skiing at Vernon Valley/Great Gorge isn't sylvan, like skiing in the remote wilds of Colorado or northern New Hampshire. An obtrusive high-tension power line cuts right down the middle of the hill, and many trails are bordered by summer amusement park equipment. But from the top, you look over miles of rolling Appalachian hills and valleys, and you can still gain the sense of freedom that comes from standing on top of the world. Some of the resort's runs are truly challenging, and some wind through the woods in an old-fashioned way. And the skiing, like skiing almost anywhere, rewards you by freeing your spirit and making your adrenalin flow.

A good place to spend a ski weekend? Yes. The amenities hold their own against facilities in many big-name destination resorts. The on-mountain spa is particularly impressive, the dining at Kite's is noteworthy, and Clement's, an authentic German brewery, provides a novel diversion, as well as some fine beer. For something a bit different, you can try winter horseback riding at the stables. On-slope special events are offered almost every week, and even the Women's Pro Racing Tour stops here.

Just down the road a piece, Hidden Valley offers a much less frenetic and more personalized atmosphere. Originally a private club, Hidden Valley has been open to the public for many years, but it retains a quiet, peaceful, out-of-the-way ambience. Most of the skiing is fairly easy and the trails are short, but the area does boast one run that is steep enough to have met international racing standards for steep pitch. The area's base lodge is home to the Alpine Chalet, a very pleasant place for a Sunday brunch.

Beginners can be introduced to skiing at Vernon/Great Gorge as I was, or at Hidden Valley, but northern New Jersey's two other alpine ski centers present the perfect introductory setting. Craigmeur is a family-owned ski hill that caters to teaching, kids, and families. Skiing here is like stopping in at a large winter picnic, especially since the people are notably friendly and happy to help. Craigmeur offers a variety of personalized learn-to-ski programs.

Campgaw, owned by the Bergen County Parks Department but privately managed, offers a touch of alpine country in the heart of suburbia. Having caught the growing snowboarding trend early, Campgaw offers one of the longest halfpipes in the east and an extremely popular snowboard park. It has become a mecca for young riders. The area also contains a Nordic ski trail that's lit for night skiing.

Along the Delaware River in Lambertville, tiny Belle Mountain is the quintessential "local" hill. But in this technological age, even the local hill is served by 100 percent snowmaking and offers night skiing.

Add them all together and it becomes clear that, yes indeed, you can ski New Jersey. Ski quite well, actually.

Specifically: Vernon Valley/Great Gorge (information: 201-827-2000; snow report: 201-579-7701; central lodging: 201-827-8815) is located in Vernon along State 94. The area is open seven days and nights and offers a variety of lift ticket options. Seasons Resort (201-827-6000 or 1-800-835-2555) offers a full slate of ski/lodging options.

Hidden Valley (information: 201-764-6161; snow report: 201-764-4200) has skiing seven days and nights a week and a full ski school.

Craigmeur (201-697-4500) is open seven days and nights and offers special lodging packages with a nearby Days Inn. Beginner lessons are offered every day.

Campgaw (201-327-7800) operates every day and night during the winter, offering several multiple day lift/lessons packages.

At Belle Mountain (609-397-0043), it's always wise to call ahead to find out what's happening.

43 Hands-on Science

Liberty Science Center

"He wants us to do what!?!" twelve-year-old Stephanie screeched. She crinkled her nose like an old candy wrapper and curled her lips like burning newspaper. "He wants you to pet the giant cockroach," I said innocently. "You're not afraid of a li'l ole cockroach, are you?" Judging by the sound that came out of her, I guess she was. She settled for staring at a "disgusting" tarantula. At least it was held safely behind glass.

Liberty Science Center in Liberty State Park brings science to life. You don't come here to "see," you come to "do." Even if some of the displays curl your lip. The museum is divided by topics, one to each floor—the environment, health, and a variety of inventions. It also holds an auditorium and one of the world's largest OmniMax film theaters.

The guy with the pet cockroach was on floor four, the environment. I wasn't squeamish. What's a roach feel like? Ah, you'll just have to go find out for yourself.

Down a flight, the kids lined up for a 3-D movie. Yep, they even wore those silly glasses. This was the health floor, site of the museum's most popular exhibit, the Touch Tunnel. It's totally dark in that tunnel. You get through by your sense of feel. But here, we ran into the museum's major problem—too crowded. The wait was an hour. No thank you.

On the invention floor you could move lasers around, make a miniature suspension bridge respond to the forces of your own weight, and work with mechanical puzzles. This floor also houses the "visiting" exhibits, some of which—like last season's "Whodunit," a murder mystery–solving challenge that explores how police use science to solve crimes—are sophisticated and extremely impressive.

With Liberty Science Center, New Jersey now has a hands-on science center that ranks with the best. Just watch those crowds. Go early on a weekend (when there are no school groups). For information, call 201-200-1000.

Thomas H. Kean Aquarium
Camden

The kids had a hard time deciding which was more exciting and scary—seeing the shark swim past right in front of your face, or actually touching the shark. True, the sharks in the large tank were safely behind glass, but they sure loomed large and dangerous! And, yes, the sharks in the touch pool were small and harmless, but (yuck! wow!) you could actually pet them!

It's hoped that the Thomas H. Kean New Jersey State Aquarium will help bring vitality back to downtown and waterfront Camden. It certainly represents a wonderful start. The facility's major attraction is a 760,000-gallon open-ocean tank, in which live more than fifty fish species. An outdoor 170,000-gallon tank houses harbor and gray seals, which are always fun to watch.

The two-floor aquarium provides a view of the undersea world usually reserved for scuba divers. A shipwreck scene on the first floor shows how man-made disaster can become viable fish habitat. Other habitats—such as waterfalls, a barrier beach, and an ocean jetty—are just as vividly re-created. Or, you can relax in the auditorium and go on a filmed exploration of even more marine habitats, like the region's rivers and bays.

Underwater life is endlessly fascinating and sometimes bizarre. Well, face it, most fish are funny-looking. That's what makes them fun. Just ask those kids over there trying to make themselves look like mantas. For information, call 609-365-3300.

JCP&L's Energy Spectrum
Forked River

Jersey Central Power & Light's Oyster Creek Plant, off Exit 74 of the Garden State Parkway, is the site of this hands-on learning center that focuses on almost all aspects of electricity. The stone-facade building is warm and welcoming, and inside you get to do everything from generating your own power to playing computer games. Information: 609-971-2100.

Jenkinson's Aquarium
Point Pleasant

Take any of the great aquaria from around the country, like the one in Camden, and shrink it down in size. Now you've got Jenkinson's. Located on the boardwalk in Point Pleasant, this collection of sea life contains a bit of everything, all very well displayed and made family-friendly by its design and its emphasis on programs for both kids and seniors. The actual sailing ship *Bounty*, from the film *Mutiny on the Bounty*, provides the decor's centerpiece (surprise! it's not full-sized), while the seal training is the major animal-oriented attraction. This is a must for all ages when at the north-central shore. Information: 908-899-1659.

New Jersey State Museum
Trenton

The State Museum does everything well – the graphic arts, the performing arts, and the sciences. The science highlight of the year comes in late January with the Super Science Weekend. That's when visitors can get together with staff and guest scientists for hands-on explorations of many scientific disciplines. The museum's planetarium presents shows and events on most weekends, including laser concerts. The Kaleidoscope

Kids program explores science, art, and history, and there are teen programs in science and the arts—even a Young Astronaut Program. For adults, there's an ongoing lecture series. The State Museum is simply a great resource. Information: 609-292-6308 or 609-292-6464.

Newark Museum
Newark
A cute, indoor mini-zoo and a planetarium highlight the Newark Museum's hands-on science facilities. Information: 201-596-6550.

Bergen Museum of Art and Science
Paramus
This is a small but dynamic museum in the heart of suburbia. Before you look in on the Hackensack mastodon and visit the science wing, call ahead for the extensive schedule of science and cultural programs for kids and adults. Information: 201-265-1248.

Trash Museum and Meadowlands Environment Center
Lyndhurst
Ever wonder what happens to that candy wrapper after you've tossed it into the garbage can? This is the place for you. In truth, everyone should visit the Trash Museum, which is filled with interactive activities, if for no other reason than to stop using the phrase "throw it away." You'll find out there is no such place as "away." You'll also get a chance to explore and learn about the surrounding urban wetlands, itself once thought to be just a nasty swamp, or a "throwaway." Information: 201-460-8300.

Monmouth Museum
Lincroft
Constantly changing exhibits are combined with participatory activities. Information: 908-747-2266.

Morris Museum
Morristown
Special events and learning opportunities abound, and there's even a live animal gallery. Request a class/event schedule for this one. Information: 201-538-0454.

Sea Life Museum
Brigantine
The Sea Life Museum houses many life-sized replicas of water animals and fish, but the museum is most notable for being the home of the Marine Mammal Stranding Center, and the story of how stranded sea life can be saved and returned to the wild makes this a compelling place to visit. Information: 609-266-0538.

Robert J. Novins Planetarium
Toms River
A full-fledged planetarium on the Ocean County College campus. Information: 908-255-4144.

Six Flags Great Adventure Safari
Jackson
Call this a "car-top wildlife experience." Located next to Great Adventure amusement park, the safari offers a realistic drive-through visit to Africa. Some 1,200 animals of sixty different species – giraffes, antelopes, tigers, camels, birds, elephants, rhinos, and more – live in this 350-acre preserve. You observe

all of them from the comfort of your own car while you listen to an informative narrative on your car radio. When the baboons use your car as a jungle gym. Information: 908-928-2000.

44 To Cross the River in Ships
New York City (and more) from Weehawken

High on Weehawken's bluffs, overlooking the Hudson River, Aaron Burr killed Alexander Hamilton in America's most infamous duel. Today, with the magnificent Manhattan skyline as a backdrop, a monument to that event stands in a pocket park along Boulevard East. Look down, rather than out, from the Hamilton monument, and you'll see a large expanse of land spreading from the cliffs' base into the Hudson. At first glance, that acreage, overgrown with weeds and cut by some derelict fencing, appears to be a no-man's-land. But look again, and you'll notice patches of activity–a golf driving range, a parking lot, and an active marina and ferryboat dock. This is Port Imperial, the home of New York Waterways.

The terminal has been fashioned from an old ferryboat and converted into a spacious, clean, and pleasantly decorated ticket office and waiting room. Next door, Arthur's Landing restaurant offers fine dining in a plush, modern atmosphere highlighted by a glass facade that reveals more of those inimitable Manhattan views. The whole complex is surrounded by formal gardens. The exotic and carefully tended plants shine against the unkempt grasses of the neighboring acreage like a diamond in a coal pile. Bordered with heritage birch trees, the gardens burst with special color-coordinated holiday displays (like red, white, and blue for July Fourth). Benches have been strategically installed to allow diners and passengers to bask in the remarkable scenic combination of exotic plants backed in one direction by the grand river and the skyscrapers, and in the other direction by the stalwart Palisades cliffs. An oasis of tranquility has been created in the heart of the surrounding bustle.

A pleasant ferry dock with a restaurant and a garden is nice, but the significance of Port Imperial lies in its easy New York City access. Frequent ferries make the crossing to Manhattan in a mere six minutes. You can travel either to midtown or the World Trade Center/Wall Street district.

The easy access offers a significant alternative for New York City tourists. Why stay in the city when you can save money lodging in New Jersey? Take, for example, a weekend of sightseeing and theater. I'd commend to your attention the Ramada Suite Hotel, located about two miles south of Port Imperial at Lincoln Harbor. An all-suites facility, with room rates considerably lower than comparable hotels in Manhattan (including much lower room tax rates), the Ramada presents more of those fantastic New Jersey–side Manhattan skyline views. On weekdays, the Lincoln Harbor ferry stops right at the hotel; on weekends, the hotel gladly drives guests to Port Imperial, a ride that takes less than five minutes.

After disembarking on the New York side, ferry riders can skip the fight for a cab or the squeeze into a bus or subway by utilizing Imperial's free shuttle mini-buses. All the major midtown and downtown attractions are easily accessible, from the aircraft carrier *Intrepid* to Rockefeller Center or Lincoln Center, and from Madison Square Garden to the Empire State Building or the World Trade Center.

Or to Broadway. Nothing tops the magic and wonder of a Broadway show. But the cost and hassle of tickets and dinner, of driving to Manhattan and parking, can be more than a little intimidating. Enter the New Jersey solution. While getting to a Broadway show from the New Jersey side can't eliminate the high ticket prices, it can reduce the other costs and eliminate many of the logistic problems. New York Waterways' "Broadway Bound" package includes dinner at Arthur's Landing, ferry across the river, and shuttle bus to the theater district. The Ramada Suite Hotel offers overnight packages, too, with show tickets included. Best of all, crossing the river by ferry adds an exotic, as well as a visually exciting appeal that driving through a tunnel just can't create.

New York Waterways can take you to more than just Manhattan. Cruises leave the ferry dock for a number of locations, including Manhattan/Liberty Island sightseeing rides and up-river guided cruises to the Tarrytown area, where you can take land tours of Washington Irving's home Sunnyside; the living seventeenth-century farm Philipsburg Manor; or the Rockefellers' extraordinary mansion Kykuit, home to a remarkable collection of sculpture and art.

In Burr and Hamilton's day, most folks who boated across the river were leaving New York City for a country idyll in provincial New Jersey. Today, sophisticated suburbanites and smart tourists are discovering that boating in the other direction is an intelligent way to start a cosmopolitan night on the town in little old New York.

Specifically: New York Waterways at Weehawken (1-800-533-3779) and Arthur's Landing Restaurant (201-867-0777) are located just north of the Lincoln Tunnel. From the Lincoln Tunnel approach, take the exit for Weehawken (marked last exit in New Jersey); go straight, bearing right at exit ramp light, and turn left at the first light onto Boulevard East. At 48th Street, turn right and go to Pershing Road.

The Ramada Suite Hotel at Lincoln Harbor (201-617-5600) can be found at 500 Harbor Boulevard in Weehawken. From the Lincoln Tunnel approach, take the exit for Weehawken (marked last exit in New Jersey); go straight, bearing right at exit ramp light, and turn right at the first light onto Boulevard East. Bear left to avoid entering the Lincoln Tunnel. At the fourth traffic light (with Dykes Lumber on the corner), turn left onto Lincoln Harbor Boulevard.

45 The Holly Walk and Other Seasonal Events, Morristown

"George Washington Slept Here!"

The phrase is heard so often in New Jersey it has become a cliché, but in Morristown, George Washington actually spent many a night. His most famous stays took place during and following Christmas. Morristown was also the longtime residence of Thomas Nast, the artist/caricaturist who created the image of Santa Claus we use today. No wonder Christmas is such a good season to go back in time at Morristown.

But beware. Christmas arrives early here. The season officially starts when Santa comes to town on the weekend before Thanksgiving. He rides in accompanied not just by a crew of reindeer or elves, but by everybody. The whole town gathers in town square, the large Christmas tree is lighted, and the season to be jolly has officially begun. After that, it's one event after another right through the end of the year.

George Washington set up shop at Morristown in January 1777, shortly after the American victories at Trenton and Princeton. Here, strategically stationed between New York and Philadelphia, the army spent the winter regrouping. After two more years of bitter fighting, they were back. That winter brought twenty-eight blizzards and was declared the worst of the century. The troops, who had little to eat, barely endured. In 1781, a rebellion among the underfed and under-clothed troops began in Morristown. It spilled headlong into Philadelphia, where the men marched on their own Congress demanding pay, food, and supplies.

Today, during the first weekend every December, the annual Holly Walk allows Morristown visitors to relive those long Revolutionary winters and voyage through the Christmas celebration styles from colonial times through the Victorian era and into the early twentieth century.

Start at the Ford Mansion and Museum, part of the National Historic Park. In addition to the colonial-era seasonal decorations, the permanent displays offer a look at military hardware and other Revolutionary period artifacts. The museum also presents a gem of a film that realistically depicts the ordeal of one common soldier during the Continental Army's second Morristown winter.

Drive next to the Wick Farm, a prosperous and spacious homesite for its time, where Gen. St. Clair headquartered during the winter of '79-'80.

Move ahead in time at Maccullouch Hall, a Federal-style mansion circa 1810 (with later improvements), and notice not only the architectural and lifestyle changes, but the variations to the way in which Christmas was celebrated and the noteworthy collection of Thomas Nast's works. A recent Maccullouch Hall Christmas display featured sleighs and other over-the-snow conveyances used in the nineteenth century.

Next, travel to the turn of the century at Fosterfields, a living history farmstead, and then on to the height of the industrial age at Historic Speedwell, the place where Samuel Morse perfected the telegraph. A few weeks prior to the Holly Walk, Speedwell Village operates a holiday crafts boutique, offering for sale an impressive variety of pieces from nearly 100 artists. The collection is good enough to merit a separate trip.

All this—the parade, the historical re-creations—are but the beginning of Christmas in Morristown.

Christmas 1920s style was a recent theme at the Morris Museum's Geraldine R. Dodge Room annual exhibit and included an eye-delighting display of mannequins attending a Jazz Age, Roaring Twenties holiday party. The display of costumes, jewelry, and Christmas ornaments was dazzling. A Victorian Christmas Lantern exhibition made up another museum exhibit.

Travel further toward the present at the Governor Morris

Hotel. In terms of historical time, the place is just a baby, built in 1962. But in its early life, the hotel was a fashionable gathering spot for fast-track New Yorkers escaping to nearby countrified-yet-sophisticated Morris County. Today, the beautifully renovated hotel celebrates the holidays with a series of lobby choral recitals by area school choirs. The music is pleasant, the kids adorable, and the setting bridges the generations, with its elaborate display of old-fashioned decorations, Continental soldiers, period-costumed mannequins, and an authentic nineteenth-century Portland Cutter sleigh.

Blooming flowers may be out of season, but the Frelinghuysen Arboretum (see Chapter 24) welcomes the season with a "Gingerbread Wonderland," a collection of structures made from gingerbread. Houses, cabins, and even whole towns are entered in the annual contest. Look, but don't taste!

Holiday concerts by the New Jersey Pops Orchestra, the Morris Choral Society, and The Masterwork Chorus are among the season's seemingly nonstop musical presentations. The nearby Paper Mill Playhouse offers *The Nutcracker* and Dickens' *A Christmas Carol.*

And just when you're feeling seasonally warm and comfy, you can remind yourself just how difficult it was to be a "common Joe" back in 1780 by joining a reenactment of the "Mutiny Hike" at Jockey Hollow National Park. Jockey Hollow is where the enlisted boys shivered hungrily through that freezing, endless winter long ago. The mutiny hike follows their rebellious route as they started for Philadelphia.

Morristown carries the seasonal celebration right through to its culminating First Night celebration (see Chapter 50).

Specifically: Morristown can be reached from the north or south via I-287, or from the east or west by State 24.

The Historic Morris Visitors Center (201 993-1194) at 14

Elm Street prints a full seasonal calendar of cultural events for the Morristown area.

For Holly Walk information, call 201-540-0211.

The Morris Museum (201-377-2982) offers ongoing permanent and rotating exhibits, classes, and special events. The museum is located at 6 Normandy Heights Road.

The Governor Morris Hotel (201-539-7300) is located at 2 Whippany Road and offers a variety of special lodging packages and dining choices. Additionally, lodging is available at The Madison Hotel (201-285-1800), Convent Road at State 24.

46 Cross-country Skiing
Fairview Lake

If you'd like to devote a day or two to cross-country skiing in New Jersey and you need to rent equipment, the Fairview Lake Ski Touring Center in Stillwater Township is the place. The only place. Many sites offer cross-country skiing; a few retailers offer rentals; but Fairview is the only place where you'll find both.

Owned and operated by the YMCA, the center offers twelve miles of marked, groomed trails; open skiing on the lake; and separate teaching area. Although the four trails are rated beginner, intermediate, and expert, Fairview will probably leave the hard-core Nordic practitioner out in the cold. For occasional hackers like me, however, the Fairview experience proved just right.

The Y runs a summer sleep-away camp here, so the entire place has that rustic, temporal feeling that only summer camp bunks and buildings can exude. After paying for our skis and trail pass at the main office, we were directed to obtain our equipment at the Program Lodge, a slightly musty and haphazardly furnished wood and stone building. The equipment keeper, a young man in his early twenties, helped us with pleasant enthusiasm. Before directing us to the ski trails, he welcomed us to "come back for hot chocolate or cider when you get cold or tired."

We embarked on an exploration of the "green" trail, the area's easiest and longest. It led us first uphill into a grove of birch and maple, then rolled along easily, an abundance of mountain laurel lining its edges. We soon established a pleasant skiing rhythm, letting the woods envelope us in a sense of freedom and quietude. There are few more pleasant feelings.

The trail ran south for perhaps a half mile, then dropped back down the hill and emptied out onto the lake. In front of us, westerly, the Kittitany Ridge, home to the Appalachian Trail, towered high above the frozen, snow-covered water, lending a wild and free sensibility. We followed the green blazes across the lake and onto the far shore. Suddenly we found ourselves gliding through a gathering of summer camp bunkhouses. It's an eerie, ghost town-ish feeling. The trail paralleled and then crossed a work road, and finished by running an exhilarating, if not all that difficult, single-track descent perched along the road's shoulder. We glided past the dining hall and back onto the lake. Altogether a pleasant run.

After a quick cider break at the lodge, I decided to take on one of the more difficult runs, the "blue" trail. Alongside the trail I noticed several numbered markers. These correspond to the summer camp's Discovery Nature Trail, for which I obtained a guide in the lodge. Since the ski trail and the nature trail weren't exactly in sync, it was sometimes difficult to follow the guide. But I still managed to identify some tree species along the way. The ski trail was relatively short, but presented me with three good downhill stretches that got my adrenaline flowing.

You can stay overnight at Fairview Lake in winterized cabins, taking family-style meals in the dining room. The center hosts a very affordable Winter Weekend Escape during mid-February, which includes meals, lodging, and activities such as indoor volleyball, movies, nature programs, sledding, and skating. Two fine bed and breakfasts offer lodging alternatives less than half an hour's drive away – Crossed Keys in Andover and the Whistling Swan Inn in Stanhope.

In abundant snow years, Nordic enthusiasts who own equipment will find excellent cross-country skiing in many parts of the state, especially in the state parks and forests. Perhaps best among them is Waywayanda State Park in the north-central reaches of Passaic County. A friend has characterized the Waywayanda skiing as "good enough to fool you into thinking you're in Vermont."

Heading cross-country on skis

But, you needn't go to the far north to enjoy backwoods sliding. The hiking trails of any state park or forest will offer good skiing. The trails of Belleplain State Park or the sand roads of Wharton State Forest provide very enjoyable skiing. Along the Delaware River, Washington's Crossing State Park is another fine skiing locale. You can even ski along the banks of the Hudson River in Palisades Interstate Park.

But, again, if you need to rent equipment, or you'd like a lesson, then Fairview Lake is for you.

Specifically: The Fairview Lake Ski Touring Center (201-383-9282) is located at 1035 Fairview Lake Road, Newton, NJ 07860. To get there coming from the east, take I-80 Exit 25 onto US 206 north into Newton, then go left onto State 94 south approximately 3.5 miles to the blinking light; go right onto County 610, which will become County 521 north; follow that into Stillwater, past the Stillwater Inn. Just beyond the elementary school on your right take an uphill left onto County 617; the center is on your left in four miles. From the west, take I-80 Exit 4 onto State 94 north; at milepost 19, you'll come to a blinking light; go left onto County 610 and follow the directions above from there.

Bed and breakfast lodging is available at the Crossed Keys in Andover (201-786-6661) and the Whistling Swan Inn in Stanhope (201-347-6369).

The New Jersey Division of Travel and Tourism's Outdoor Guide lists the state parks and forests that offer marked Nordic ski trails; call 1-800-537-7397 for a copy.

47 A Holiday House Tour
Spring Lake

When you climb the front steps of the Carriage House, a classic nineteenth-century vacation "cottage" by the sea, Santa greets you on the wrap-around porch with a belly laugh. His helper elf offers a candy morsel and with a hearty "Merry Christmas!" they welcome you to go inside.

In the living room, you melt into the warmth. Christmas music plays quietly, an innocent mechanized angel dances a small pirouette atop a beautifully garnished Christmas tree, a delicious yuletide aroma – a titillating mix of orange, cinnamon, and cloves – emanates from the large kitchen, and each nook and cranny of the inn houses an enticing seasonal decoration. Welcome to the Spring Lake Christmas Hospitality Tour.

The beauty of Spring Lake is its quiet simplicity. It's a pastoral, *Our Town* kind of a place, with wide tree-lined streets, large, well-kept period homes set in manicured yards, an inviting mini-downtown four blocks long, a meticulously kept oceanfront, and, of course, the two gem-like, underground spring–fed lakes (well, okay, some would call them ponds) that give the village its name. When film director Milos Forman went looking for a place to set his movie version of *Ragtime*, an early-twentieth-century period piece, he chose Spring Lake.

Spring Lake entices visitors with one of the finest bed and breakfast collections in the state. The Hospitality Tour, organized on the first weekend of December, offers an opportunity to see a handful of these hostelries dressed in their holiday finest.

Each bed and breakfast reflects the personality and tastes of its owners. At the Carriage House, Santa's elf is really seventeen-year-old Patty Ogletree, daughter of the proprietors, and Santa is her schoolmate Tim. Hostess Fran Ogletree has put out cookies on the kitchen table and peppered the place with Christmas images. Here, on a neat little stairway windowsill, a miniature

Santa rides his tiny sleigh on a bed of white styrofoam snow; up there, in the first of the upstairs bedrooms, a three-foot, handmade angel welcomes visitors.

A few blocks away at La Maison, Barbara Furdyna has created a French country home theme. "Père Noel" (Santa), wearing wooden clogs and carrying a miniature basket filled with tiny traditional champagne bottles, stands atop the coffee table in the sitting room. Wooden clogs, the French equivalent of Christmas stockings, are set by the fireplace waiting to be filled with presents. Across the hall, a traditional "bouche de Noel"–a rich chocolate Yule log cake–and two real bottles of champagne adorn the main dining table, while standing to one side, a classic creche (nativity scene) features "santons," figures depicting working-class people, surrounding the manger.

Barbara's home was built in 1870 and has functioned as an inn since day one. She greets tour visitors in her parlor and explains to them the history of the house and how, in her renovations, she has carried out the French theme. She cheerfully reveals why her Christmas tree is adorned with glittering fish (a tradition of seaside southern France), and welcomes you to browse through the crafts she offers for sale.

At Victoria House, you enter a Victorian period piece that has been painstakingly and artfully restored by Louise and Robert Goodall. Before your eye is dazzled by the ten-foot living room Christmas tree, take notice of the new tin ceiling in the entry foyer; then, follow the garlands that travel up the staircase to admire the guest rooms' decor. Louise will tell you she has had no professional decorating experience, but it's hard to believe. As you exit through the kitchen, stop at least long enough to appreciate the hand-carved antique chairs.

Hollycroft presents an altogether different face. Set back from the street, you follow a twisting driveway and suddenly find yourself outside a log-and-stucco fairy-tale cottage. The house, proprietors Mark and Linda Fessler will gladly tell you, was built in 1908 in the arts and crafts style. The simple wood-and-log-beam construction was a reaction to the opulent Victorian-era tastes. The Fesslers have garlanded their intriguing lodge with an array of decorations, including an eye-catching collection of grapevine figurines. Each room has its own miniature lighted tree, and Christmas music pervades the open, rustic, but richly decorated dining room, living room, and brick-floored breakfast room on the main floor. The Fesslers, too, offer seasonal crafts for sale.

The tour ends with afternoon tea at the grand oceanside Warren Hotel. A perfect finish, unless you've been astute enough to book a room for the weekend in order to attend a performance of *Scrooge* at the Community House. This polished, annual community theater offering features, as one innkeeper put it, "just about every kid in town and adult residents who have been playing their parts for years."

As long as you're staying for the show, you may as well go downtown to shop. The museum-like Vitale & Vitale is a must-see; the collection of clocks, displayed in a neo-classical environment, immerses you in the world of timepieces. The art and history of each functional and collectible clock is explained in a gallery setting that makes it easy to forget you're in a shop. You'll also enjoy sampling the handmade candies at Jean Louise's, browsing among the Irish goods at the Irish Centre, as well as visiting the unique toy and antique shops.

A small fee is charged to participate in the Hospitality Tour, all the proceeds of which go to charity. And, by the way, if you can't make it in December, a springtime tour takes place in early June.

Specifically: To reach Spring Lake, take the Garden State Parkway to Exit 34 south and follow State 34 south to the first traffic circle; follow the circle three-quarters of the way around, and get on County 524 east; or from I-195 east, exit at State 34 south and do the same.

Spring Lake can also be reached by train on the New Jersey Transit Coast Line (201-460-8444), or by bus from New York City's Port Authority Bus Terminal (212-564-8484). Call for schedule information.

The Christmas Hospitality Tour takes place during the first weekend in December; for tour and general information call 908-449-0577.

For information and lodging rates for the bed and breakfasts noted above, call: La Maison, 908-449-0969; Carriage House, 908-449-1332; Victoria House, 908-974-1882; Hollycroft Inn, 908-681-2254.

48 Through a Glass Brightly
Wheaton Village at Christmas, Millville

While Bing Crosby's singing of "White Christmas" may touch something deep within all of us, in south central New Jersey it's not snow but sand that holds sway. South Jerseyans have long spun that sand into glass in both practical and fanciful shapes. And nowhere is there a better celebration of glass in all its manifestations than in Millville's Wheaton Village.

We ventured to the American Museum of Glass during the holiday season to view the annual Christmas exhibit. The theme, which changes each year, was "Christmas in New Jersey." A series of lifesized scenes depicted Christmas celebrations and decorations from different New Jersey times and places, including "Caroling in Hackensack, 1898" (complete with recorded musical accompaniment), and a portrayal of the "Millville Christmas Parade, 1949." The museum's lobby, a re-creation of Cape May's Mainstay Hotel at the turn of the century, was dominated by an enormous Christmas tree.

Wheaton's Christmas exhibit is carefully researched and inventively created; it adds an appealing sense of historical depth to our celebration of the season. In truth, however, the museum deserves a visit at any time of year. The place houses one of the largest glass collections in the country and displays it beautifully in four wings constituting nearly 20,000 square feet of exhibition space.

Progressing through the museum means traveling through time, beginning with early New Jersey glass pieces. The bottle room includes bottles designed to hold everything from soda and perfume to patent medicines, ink, and milk for babies. Just making bottles for bitters, we learned, was at one time an $80 million industry.

Other exhibitions include art glass, a re-created Victorian kitchen, a New Jersey Room that features the work of local companies and artists, a research library, and a Paperweight Room.

Paperweights hold a place of special importance at Wheaton Village and among glass enthusiasts. Behind the museum, at the re-created T. C. Wheaton Glass Factory, paperweight-making demonstrations are almost always under way. The Creative Glass Center of America offers a select number of artists' fellowships to glassmakers, and these resident artists are among the craftspeople who demonstrate their techniques for the public. The factory was constructed in 1972 as a replica of Wheaton's 1888 building. The main furnace is surrounded by a spectators' gallery from which visitors can watch narrated demonstrations. Usually these presentations include the creation of a paperweight and a piece of blown glass. If you'd like to purchase a paperweight, take a short walk back to the village's main street, and stop in at the Arthur Gorham Paperweight Shop.

Six shops and an art gallery line the main walkway. Here a variety of items – books, jewelry, crafts, collectibles, and, of course, glass of all sorts – are available for purchase. The nineteenth-century village certainly is pretty, and it attains a quaint antique effect, albeit with a bit of a touristy overlay. More effective is the earthy Crafts and Trades Row, a rough, long building (kind of pieced together in three sections) that houses working craftspeople, including a potter; a lampworker, who works cold glass into decorations; and a woodcarver, who works in an environment celebrating southern New Jersey's maritime tradition. Next door, in a building that features a classic three-hole privy, a tinsmith demonstrates his craft.

Other Wheaton Village installations include a railroad station with a half-scale steam train ride that circles the village, an 1876 schoolhouse, and a print shop.

Modern Millville, home to the worldwide Wheaton Glass Company, remains an international glassmaking capital, a role it has filled for a long time. Wheaton Village wonderfully expresses that history and spirit.

Specifically: Millville and Wheaton Village are reached via State 55; exit at State 49 and follow the signs.

Wheaton Village (609-825-6800 or 1-800-998-4552) is open from 10:00 A.M. till 5:00 P.M. every day, and until 8:00 P.M. on Wednesdays. The Christmas exhibit is displayed from just after Thanksgiving until just after New Year. For a year-round calendar of events, call or write Wheaton Village, Wade Boulevard, Millville, NJ 08332.

Lodging is available next door at Country Inn by Carlson; for information or reservations, call 609-825-3100 or 1-800-456-4000.

49 Washington's Crossing and the Battles of Trenton, Trenton

"How long does it take Washington to cross the Delaware?" I asked, sounding as if I was giving a set-up line for a joke.

"About five or ten minutes," replied the lady from the Washington's Crossing State Park. "Fifteen at the most."

Amazing. Back in 1776, Washington required all night to get across the river.

"You really want to get down here at least an hour or more before the crossing," she warned me generously. "That's when he inspects and addresses the troops. And besides, if you get here any later than that, you'll have to park at least a mile away."

Ah, George. Aren't you glad all you had to worry about was sub-zero cold, ice choking the river, operating with stealth in the dark of night, and boosting the rapidly sinking morale of your ragged troops? You never had to suffer the consequences of limited parking.

Washington's Crossing and the Battles of Trenton represent a major turning point in the birthing of our nation. Prior to Trenton, Washington and his beleaguered troops were being vilified as capable only of retreat. These reenactments are even more special because they are faithfully held on their actual anniversaries – Christmas Day and December 26th – no matter how inconvenient that may be.

Crossing festivities begin with several screenings of a half-hour documentary film in the Memorial Building on the Pennsylvania side of the river and with a display featuring the famous painting by Emanuel Leutze entitled (appropriately enough) "Washington Crossing the Delaware." Promptly at 2:00 P.M., more than 100 soldiers march one block from the McConkey Ferry Inn to the river, where Washington addresses the troops, and then they climb into authentic reproduction Durham boats for the cross-river row. After landing in New Jersey, the soldiers march to the John Honeyman Monument to pay their respects to the man who spied on the Hessians that night and gave Washington the information he needed to attack and win.

On December 26, 1776, after encountering many unexpected delays, Washington managed to surprise the Hessians in Trenton. On December 26, 1993, we, too, encountered delays – a mysterious back-up on the New Jersey Turnpike. Times change, delays change. We managed to arrive at Trenton's Old Barracks Museum just as the troops were hopping into their pick-up trucks and minivans to head out for the fight.

We quickly followed. We could hear the distant sound of drums, and saw the occasional costumed soldier running on the next block. We even heard shots.

No sooner had we joined the other spectators at Mill Hill Park than the troops arrived. Standing in the bitter wind that whistled through the streets of Trenton that day and looking at this close approximation of the colonists' actual dress – woolen uniforms and knickers, leather boots and three-cornered hats (gloves optional) – evoked a sense of awe at their hardiness. It's a wonder they didn't all die of exposure within that winter's first week.

Awe soon gave way to confusion. Some men were dressed in the expected British red coats, but others were in green. Hessians? Still others were in blue. It was impossible to tell the soldiers without a scorecard. The Americans seemed to be in retreat instead of taking the Brits by surprise.

Just as the cold-ache in our toes began to turn to numbness, the firing suddenly ceased. After light applause, one of the soldiers faced the crowd and began to explain what we had just seen: the *second* Battle of Trenton. Hold it! You mean there were two of them? Yes. Buoyed by reinforcements, the British made an attempt to get even with Washington's boys several days after the surprise attack. They fought to a stand-off.

It turns out that our Turnpike traffic jam had caused us to miss the *first* Battle of Trenton. I guess we should have come by Durham boat.

That explained, everyone quickly retreated back to the Old Barracks Museum – the soldiers to act out a Retreat Ceremony that would officially end their day's work, most of us spectators to get inside, where it was warm.

Trenton offers a treasure trove of historical sites. The Old Barracks Museum was originally constructed in 1758 as one of five buildings to house British soldiers who, in the colonies to fight the French and Indian War, had been lodging in the colonists' homes – whether the homeowners welcomed them or not. The building is the last existing colonial-period barracks, and it houses permanent and changing exhibits illustrating colonial life, as well as a tour with a guide who describes life in America circa 1777.

The William Trent House was built in 1719 on a 1,600-acre estate by the man who laid out what he called Trent's Town. Mr. Trent's house was later home to three New Jersey governors. It has been restored to its eighteenth-century resplendence and boasts a noteworthy collection of William and Mary–style furniture. Guided tours are offered daily.

The Trenton City Museum is located in an 1848, thirty-four-room Tuscan villa called Ellarslie. The building houses a large collection of art and historical objects. On the second floor, you can learn about Trenton's past role as a pottery and manufacturing center. Also on display is a particularly fascinating series of paintings, commissioned for the 1939 New York World's Fair, depicting life in the John A. Roebling's Sons wire rope factory, which made the cables for the famous Brooklyn Bridge.

The New Jersey State Museum must be counted among the state's finest resources, offering displays and programs relating to archeology, cultural history, natural history, and contemporary and classical art. The museum holds a 150-seat planetarium and offers hands-on science programs for families and school groups (see Chapter 43). It also hosts student workshops in writing and the performing arts, as well as special events such as the Super Science Weekend.

Downtown Trenton offers art galleries, more historical buildings, and a number of good restaurants. And of course, since Trenton is New Jersey's capital city, visitors can watch the state legislature in action—when it is in session, and when the visitors are not stuck in traffic or rowing across the Delaware!

Specifically: Washington's Crossing is reenacted every Christmas Day, beginning at noon. Call 215-493-4076 for directions and information.

Events and ceremonies for the Battles of Trenton run from 11:00 A.M. to 3:00 P.M. on December 26th. A narrated walking tour of the battle is offered at 2:00 P.M. Call 609-396-1776.

The Old Barracks Museum (609-396-1776), located on Barrack Street, is open from Tuesday through Sunday; call for hours and holiday closings.

The William Trent House (609-989-3027) is at 15 Market Street; it's open from 10:00 A.M. to 2:00 P.M. daily, but closed on major holidays.

Ellarslie, the Trenton City Museum (609-989-3632), is in Cadwalader Park, and has hours from Tuesday through Sunday, but is closed on major holidays.

The New Jersey State Museum (609-292-6308) is at 205 West State Street; it operates from Tuesday through Sunday and is closed for holidays. Call for a schedule of events.

The Trenton Downtown Association prints a useful map and guide to the city's downtown attractions; write to Trenton Downtown Association, 23 East State Street, Trenton, NJ 08608.

50 Christmas with the Dickenses – The Hermitage, Ho-Ho-Kus

It's a cold December evening, just perfect for visiting friends in their warm and cheerfully decorated home. So you drive over to visit the Dickenses at the large stone house with the steep, wood-shingled roof, pinnacled dormers, and gingerbread trim. As you step across the threshold, you not only receive a cordial welcome, but you pass through time as well. You've entered the world of master novelist Mr. Charles Dickens, circa 1843.

Mr. Dickens and family greet you graciously, but urgency is in the air. For tonight, Charles will be sharing his newest work, specially written for the holidays. He calls it *A Christmas Carol*. Dickens can't wait to read it to you. As he does, other family members and friends will act out the parts. After this thoroughly amusing Victorian tradition (they call it parlor theater), everyone will move to the dining room, where the Dickenses will be serving hot cider and an odd concoction they call "Smoking Bishop." It's made with wine, oranges, cloves, and sugar.

"Christmas Dickens" has become a holiday custom at The Hermitage, the only eighteenth/nineteenth century Bergen County house to be designated a national landmark. Dickens' *A Christmas Carol*, relating as it does the miraculous personal salvation undergone by Scrooge, is somehow particularly appropriate here. The Hermitage, too, represents something of a miraculous deliverance. All done up for the holiday season, with authentic Victorian ornaments, pine roping, garlands across the ceiling, gilding everywhere, and a "kissing ball" (mistletoe, berries, ivy, and holly entwined) hanging from above, it's hard to imagine that for years this magnificent home was the scariest place in suburbia. But it was.

The Hermitage was first built about 1750 as a two-story Georgian house along the New York–Albany post road. Owners Col. James Marcus and Mrs. Theodosia Prevost hosted George

Washington here for a celebration weekend shortly after the American victory at the Battle of Monmouth. Theodosia was widowed in 1780, but she remarried in the house in 1782 – to one Aaron Burr, future vice president of the United States and victor over Alexander Hamilton in the country's most infamous duel.

In 1807, The Hermitage was purchased by Dr. Elijah Rosencranz, one of the first physicians to reside in the area. Dr. Rosencranz then built a highly successful cotton mill on nearby Ho-Ho-Kus Brook. The Rosencranzes remodeled the house significantly during the mid-nineteenth century. Most of the original home was leveled, and the Victorian gothic design we see today was created. For its time, the home was state-of-the-art, with such advanced technology as indoor plumbing, central heating, and closets, at a time when most homes had only wardrobes.

The house stayed in the Rosencranz family for more than a century and a half. But by the 1960s, the building had deteriorated badly. The lone surviving family member, Mary Elizabeth Rosencranz, and her companion, Kathryn Zahner, lived there in near-poverty, occupying only one of the home's nineteen rooms. Still, Elizabeth refused many lucrative offers for the 4.9-acre property and upon her death in 1970, the house and grounds were willed to the state. By then The Hermitage was known among the neighborhood kids as "the Ghost House." If this place wasn't something right out of *The Addams Family*, then nothing was. I remember well the derelict, "haunted" house on Franklin Turnpike from my own high school days. "What is that place?" we'd ask as we cruised by on a Saturday night. None of us knew.

Luckily, there were people who did know, not only what that place was, but how valuable it could be. They formed an organization called the Friends of The Hermitage and set about

Spend a Victorian Christmas at The Hermitage

restoring it to its former grandeur. The Friends have brought back the luster and made The Hermitage into a living museum. They have developed an impressive archive that includes more than 10,000 items—textiles, period clothing, photographs (mostly taken by the shutter-happy Rosencranz family), letters, maps, and historical documents that were found on the premises. The collection has made The Hermitage into a vital regional historical resource.

The Friends draw on those resources to create events and raise support funds, which is how you might find yourself enjoying a number of activities there. In addition to an evening of Christmas parlor theater with Charles Dickens, you can participate in a Victorian dinner party "whodunit" murder mystery in the spring; attend a symposium on the Victorian era and a Victorian fashion show; shop at the twice-yearly crafts shows, or just drop by on a Sunday afternoon for a docent-led tour at The Hermitage's small café in the smaller, adjacent, 1892 John Rosencranz House.

History buffs can combine a Hermitage visit with stops at two important nearby sites. There's the Steuben House in Hackensack, a sandstone home on the banks of the Hackensack River that dates from the early 1700s, and serves now as a museum of early Dutch-American culture and as the headquarters for the Bergen County Historical Society. And you can also explore Lambert Castle, the elegant, 1892, Belle Vista residence of silk manufacturer Catholina Lambert, built atop Garrett Mountain overlooking downtown Paterson.

The Hermitage is yet another New Jersey treasure that is too easily overlooked. It took me more than twenty years to stop in. It won't be long before I return.

Specifically: The Hermitage (201-445-8311), at 335 North Franklin Turnpike in Ho-Ho-Kus, can be reached from Exit 165 of the Garden State Parkway; take Ridgewood Avenue west (toward Ridgewood), continuing into downtown Ridgewood; turn right onto Maple Avenue, and go about 1.5 miles to Franklin Turnpike (Claude's Ho-Ho-Kus Inn will be in front of you); go left, and The Hermitage will be on the left side in about half a mile. Call for tour and event schedules.

For information on the Steuben House, call 201-487-1739; for Lambert Castle, call 201-881-2761.

51 First Night
Montclair

As a freshman in college, I spent New Year's Eve at Times Square, sideways drunk. When I awoke on New Year's Day, the ringing pain in my head said, "There's got to be a better way."

There is.

On that same New Year's Eve, 1967, a group of folks in Boston were creating it. They called their celebration First Night. The idea was to forget the alcohol and spend the evening in a more meaningful celebration, with art exhibits, musical performances, theater, and dance. There are currently some 120 First Night celebrations in North America; New Jersey hosts more than any other state.

First Night came to New Jersey in 1987 at Montclair. Suburban in nature, the town nevertheless harbors an active cultural, arts, and performance community. In addition to the excellent Montclair Museum, there's an international array of restaurants, several music clubs, and a professional theater. Numerous professional musicians and performers live here. For a relatively small suburb, Montclair is downright cosmopolitan.

By New Year's Eve 1994, First Night Montclair drew 14,000 people. We went to see why.

Darkness fell, and so did the rain. It wasn't a severe rainfall, more like a heavy mist. We momentarily reconsidered our New Year's plans.

"What happens to a festival in which you walk around town when it rains?" we wondered.

The answer was–nothing. The show goes on.

Celebrants circulated through the town, never missing a beat; they just put their umbrellas up and down as the weather demanded. We joined right in.

First Night Montclair takes place at some thirty-three venues, ranging from school auditoriums to churches to the Montclair Museum. Choosing among the dozens of events is the hardest part. We started with a visit to the George Innis Theater at the high school, mostly because we were standing right there when it was time for jazz singer Jeannie Bryson to take the stage. Between numbers, people wandered in and out as they pleased. They were coming from and leaving for other venues. The informal quality was much like being at a party and breaking off a conversation in one room to see someone in the next. Only here, the next room could be several blocks away, or across town.

We left Ms. Bryson after a handful of songs and wandered down Park Street, a street bordered by huge houses and lined with large trees. We were heading downtown, but we were attracted to musical sounds emanating from the Central Presbyterian Church. We ducked inside. The New Jersey Children's Choir was performing. A baby cried incessantly. A girl in the choir's second row dealt with a perpetual nose itch. But the large room offered fantastic acoustics, and the kids sounded just fine as they finished with a moving chorus of "Should auld acquaintance be forgot. . . ."

The room emptied. We consulted our schedules. If we began hoofing it right away, we could get up to Montclair Academy in time to see the stand-up comics. I love stand-up comics. We walked. By the time we made it up the Bloomfield Avenue hill (which took a while), we were walking in a crowd.

The lobby was choked with folks waiting. We poked our heads into the Academy's auditorium. On stage, two or three dozen kids and a few young adults were dancing with pure youthful exuberance. We took seats. To an upbeat and moving lyric that said "We are one," the troupe filled the auditorium with life. *Ceremony in Dance* is an event created especially for First Night through a program that places professional performers in the local middle school to work with the kids. The energy alone made the show wonderful to watch.

Ceremony in Dance was followed by the stand-up comics. They drew an SRO crowd. It wasn't raucous, like a nightclub, and the humor was pretty clean, but it was funny. These guys were doing two shows, and the crowd outside when we left looked bigger than our crowd. Good luck finding seats.

We loped back down the hill and hurried into the Montclair Museum in an effort to see the Silk City Quartet, an eclectic string band that combines country sounds with klezmer, swing, bluegrass, and Brazilian music. Alas, we reached the door just in time to be told there was no more room.

Continuing down the hill, we came across a church that literally rocked with revivalist singing. A combo—electric piano, a priest on sax, and a full complement of trumpets, drums, trombones, and singers—had folks dancing in the aisles. We'd been looking for a magician who was scheduled for a performance at a bank. Distracted, we never made it. Indeed, we never made it to half the things we'd have found interesting—the sky show at the school planetarium, the ice show at the skating rink, the square dancing at the high school, the paper-cutting demo on the promenade, the New Jersey Chamber Music Society at the First Congregational Church . . . .

You get the idea.

We got the idea, too. A community at one, all ages, bidding adieu to the old year, welcoming the new, enjoying each other's joys and talents. It sure beat being drunk at Times Square.

Specifically: In 1994, New Jersey hosted about ten First Night Celebrations; in 1995 at least twenty are expected to be staged. Among them: Maplewood/South Orange, Morristown, Ocean City, Red Bank, Summit, Teaneck, Toms River, Caldwell, Woodbridge, and there's even one at the Garden State Plaza Shopping Center in Paramus. To obtain a list of New Jersey First Nights, call Paul Ellis at 201-509-4910.

52 Cabin Fever Cure: The Garden State Flower and Garden Show, Somerset

The skies hung a heavy gray. The thermometer was dropping, and the weatherman warned of yet another snowstorm. The ice had congealed on the ground long enough to grow dirty and mean. Although we were all prepared to turn the calendar to March, warm weather couldn't have seemed farther away. What better time to thumb your nose at the cold? What better way to do that than by tiptoeing through thousands of tulips?

I gathered up my mom and headed for the New Jersey Flower and Garden Show, staged annually at the Garden State Exhibit Hall in Somerset, Franklin Township. The hall is located in a commercial complex that seemed an unlikely site to celebrate nature. Parking is tight, and traffic backs up easily. But we regarded seriously the admonition to get there early and encountered no delay; I can't say that for those who arrived later.

To enter the Garden and Flower Show was to travel instantly from a gray winter's day to a bright, warm, springtime afternoon bathed in a color riot. Each year, the show centers on a theme. This time it was "400 Years of Garden Magic," featuring the "gardens from the Netherlands." It seems that 1994 marked the 400th anniversary of the first planting of tulips in the Netherlands. In those 400 years, people have developed a lot of tulip varieties, some 3,500 of them, of which 900 are currently commercially available. The show itself featured 100 tulip cultivars represented by some 120,000 individual plants, each of them equally as remarkable and beautiful as the next.

We learned a lot about tulips. We learned, for example, that the Dutch preserve the great tulips of the past in a special garden—ten of those antique bulbs were exhibited at the New Jersey show; we learned that it takes fifteen to twenty-five years to bring a new tulip variety to market—forty-two new cultivars, each not quite yet ready for market (being two to five years away), were on display; and we learned that seventeenth-century Dutchmen paid up to $1,500 for a single tulip bulb.

Our education was by no means limited to tulips. Tucked in the far corner of the hall, hidden behind some dreary dark-green cloth room dividers, we visited the Seeds of Knowledge Education Center. Over the ten-day course of the show, the center hosted some fifteen seminars, their topics ranging from "Edible Flowers" to "Computer-Aided Landscape Design." Guest speakers and seminars were slotted daily into the noon to 1:00 P.M. and 3:00 to 4:00 P.M. slots. On closing weekend, Joel Rapp, who bills himself as "Mr. Mother Earth" and serves as the gardening editor of the "Live with Regis and Kathie Lee" TV show, was slated to appear. His topic? Container gardening. Other featured speakers included Patricia Taylor, author of *Easy Care Shade Gardening,* and photographer Walter Choroszewski, who presented a slide show from his book *The Garden State in Bloom.* Ralph Snodsmith, gardening editor of "Good Morning America!" and WOR-Radio garden show host, appears every year.

We happened to wander into the Education Center between guest speakers and found guest floral designers who displayed their skills three times daily. Designers created arrangements while a moderator dissected and explained their work. It was a little like medical students watching surgeons in an operating theater, with the added pandemonium of browsers and showgoers rattling noisily in the background. The designers we watched produced arrangements as if it were a race, but the moderator analyzed their work at a leisurely pace. When the analysis was over, the subject arrangement was put up for sale at half its stated retail value. The presentation fascinated. How often do we get to watch professional artists at work, actually developing their creations before our eyes?

Fascinating in another way was the array of exhibitors in what was euphemistically called the "Market Fair" area. These

A breath of spring at the flower show

guys ranged from the nonprofit Isles, Inc. (an organization that develops inner-city community gardens) and the New Jersey Native Plant Society to commercial enterprises of all kinds. The presence of some vendors seemed logical, but I was baffled by the participation of some others. Flower show-goers get information on everything from garden and home centers to deck makers and solarium manufacturers, or they can shop for such items as pussy willows from Rosy's Pussy Ranch, vegetable choppers, the *Encyclopaedia Britannica,* or a subscription to the New York *Times.* It was great fun to stroll the aisles and watch the vendors at work.

Exiting, one more survey of the flowers and display gardens provided a last dazzling burst of sunlight and color and a refreshing glimpse of spring's bounty as we'd soon enjoy it – outdoors. It was all a tease, of course. One woman, while waiting by the exit for her senior citizens' group bus, looked gloomily into the wind-swirling snow that had begun falling during our stay. "Oh well," she said. "Back to reality."

Specifically: The Garden State Flower and Garden Show (908-919-7660) is a nonprofit endeavor staged at the end of February and early March. The Garden State Exhibit Hall can be reached by taking I-287 to Exit 6 and following the signs. Show hours are 10:00 A.M. to 9:00 P.M., Monday through Saturday, 10:00 A.M. to 6:00 P.M. on Sundays, and 4:00 to 9:00 P.M. on the opening Friday. Admission is charged, but children under twelve are admitted free with a paying adult; group rates apply to advance purchases for parties of ten or more.

Index